THE
5 ESSENTIAL
PEOPLE SKILLS

Also available from Dale Carnegie Training

Leadership Mastery

THE
5 ESSENTIAL
PEOPLE SKILLS

How to Assert Yourself,
Listen to Others, and
Resolve Conflicts

DALE CARNEGIE
TRAINING

**SIMON &
SCHUSTER**

London · New York · Sydney · Toronto

A CBS COMPANY

First published in Great Britain in 2009 by Simon & Schuster UK Ltd
This paperback edition published by Simon & Schuster UK Ltd, 2012
A CBS COMPANY

3 5 7 9 10 8 6 4 2

Simon & Schuster UK Ltd
1st Floor
222 Gray's Inn Road
London
WC1X 8HB

www.simonandschuster.co.uk

Simon & Schuster Australia, Sydney
Simon & Schuster India, New Delhi

A CIP catalogue copy for this book is available
from the British Library.

ISBN: 978-1-47111-524-0

Printed and bound in India by Replika Press Pvt. Ltd.

Contents

Preface

Dale Carnegie has done more than perhaps any other person to change the field of human relations and personal development. His world-famous program, *The Dale Carnegie Course*, has helped literally millions of people.

Looking back on his early years, Mr. Carnegie saw that worry and fear were the two forces that prevented him from achieving his own personal success. Conquering these two self-defeating emotions brought Mr. Carnegie a new perspective and new success. As a result, he made it his mission to help others overcome worry and fear so they could achieve their dreams.

Now, with this book, you too can benefit from the nine decades of insights into human relations that millions of people have discovered from Dale Carnegie Training. After experiencing *The 5 Essential People Skills: How to Assert Yourself, Listen to Others, and Resolve Conflicts*, you'll gain the ability to focus on the factors that will move you and your organization forward. You'll discover and be able to apply these proven practices, which will assist you in feeling empowered, respected, and at ease in any business or personal communication. They will improve your confidence while training you in the ways to get your message across with greater esteem, power, and clarity.

The primary achievement of this book is to identify and explore five essential people skills: **rapport building, curiosity, communication, ambition, conflict resolution**. But this is really just the beginning. As you'll see, a number of chapters extend and develop the five skills in new and exciting directions. So, as you move through these pages, be flexible in your thinking and proactive in applying the information you gain. Starting right now!

To achieve maximum benefits from this book, don't procrastinate. We suggest that you simply devote five minutes (or more) to begin reading. As you proceed through the book, be sure to complete the Action Steps section at the end of each chapter. These exercises are practical steps you can take immediately—in your work or with your family and friends.

Whenever possible, give yourself a deadline, and hold yourself accountable for following through on that deadline. If you do not implement the action steps that you have mapped out for yourself, this book simply becomes an exercise in reading. While this is definitely effective, you will gain the full benefits that this valuable book has to offer you by working through the action steps. Make the life-changing choice to act upon your insights, ideas, and strategies, and you will achieve results that you never dreamed of.

Gain strength from the positive and don't be sapped by the negative.

—Dale Carnegie

CHAPTER 1

An Introduction to Assertiveness

Just over seventy years ago, Dale Carnegie published a book that remains one of the most influential works of the past hundred years. What's more, it will probably be one of the most influential in the next century as well. That book is called *How to Win Friends and Influence People.* The title could not be much clearer, could it? The ideas that it contains are every bit as clear, and as valid, today as they were in 1936, when the book first appeared. Although *How to Win Friends and Influence People* is a monumental document in the history of personal development, it was a true groundbreaker when it first appeared. Before the publication of Dale Carnegie's book, the whole concept of people skills didn't really exist. Yet today we take it for granted that some approaches are better than others in human interactions.

Dale Carnegie's book put forth timeless human relations principles that remain essential today. In fact, their influence is greater than ever before. With the advance in technology and the speed of business, those who master interpersonal skills not only are a greater asset in today's workplace but achieve greater success. Computers and cell phones have made a big difference in our lives, but the importance of effective people skills has not diminished and it never will.

It really is impossible, however, to discuss a topic like people skills (especially in a business environment) without referring to the Internet, cell phones, and emails. These things are everywhere. Where you go, they go. The new technologies have certainly sped up the way things get done in the modern workplace, but they've also raised the expectations of how fast things need to get done. Today, people don't say they need something done tomorrow. They need it "yesterday." It's strange but true, and it's also something of a paradox. Work in many ways has become easier and faster, but work-related tensions are probably higher than ever before. Stress is everywhere and always—and we all know that when tensions are high, the potential for friction between individuals rises proportionately.

This is the reality we're living in. There's no getting around it. This is the environment in which we must learn to succeed. And when I say "we," I mean "you," no matter who you are or what your career path might be. It doesn't really matter what area of the economy we are in, because the same forces are at play everywhere. So you'd better get on board. Dale Carnegie said it very well: "No matter what your line of work, even if it's in one of the technical professions, your degree of success depends on your ability to interact effectively with other people." Despite the fact that the technical professions are now the most potent sector of the American economy, those words still hold true.

EXPLORATION AND SELECTION

In the chapters that follow, we're going to be looking closely at exactly what's involved in assertive interactions. Our exploration will be quite selective. We've deliberately tried to make the subjects covered in this book very specific and sharply focused. The purpose here is not to say everything but to say a relatively small number of things very well. There are already fine books on the market dealing with conventional topics like effective listening or the keys to making a good sales presentation. But why cover ground that's been thoroughly explored? Instead, we're going to be looking at new areas, including five in particular: rapport building, curiosity, communication, ambition, and conflict resolution—plus other topics that are natural extensions of these.

But there is one aspect of people skills that can never really receive enough attention, because it's the foundation of every kind of effective human interaction.

We're referring to assertiveness: the ability to speak and act in ways that naturally cause people to respond attentively and positively. It is the basic core element that is at the center of each of the five essential people skills. If you're not prepared to assert yourself in a positive and proactive manner, nothing else can possibly happen. So let's begin by looking at the real meaning of assertiveness in today's work environment—where you really must make yourself stand out in order to get any attention at all. As this discussion goes on, we'll see how assertiveness differs from other, less effective forms of interaction.

There are a few things we can take for granted. Every human being, for example, has the desire to be treated fairly. We may not feel like fairness is happening, but at least fairness is something we want. What's more, when we feel we are not being treated fairly, we should insist on being treated fairly. We shouldn't just roll over on our backs and play dead, although that's more or less what many people do. To be treated fairly we must clearly, tactfully, and effectively express our preferences, needs, opinions, grievances, and other feelings. Nobody else should have to do this on our behalf. We have a responsibility to express our own needs. We also have a further responsibility to do so in an appropriate and productive way. If we don't do that, we are not only depriving ourselves of what we deserve, we are also depriving the people around us of the real contributions we have to make.

PUTTING OUR RIGHTS AND RESPONSIBILITIES INTO ACTION

Establishing reasonable parameters for being treated fairly is what assertiveness really means. These are like traffic laws: Getting where you want to go is important, but that doesn't mean you can run all the red lights. Assertiveness is the middle ground between the two extremes of reckless aggressiveness and defeatist passivity. The genuinely assertive person is neither one of these. Aggressive people are self-centered, inconsiderate, hostile, and arrogantly demanding. They drive people away. Passive people are weak, compliant, and disrespectful of his or her own best interests. They also drive others away—except perhaps for aggressive people! Between these two poles, however, are people who know how to make their ideas known without preventing others from doing likewise. Your task is to become one of those people. Men and women who can do that are assertive people, and the purpose of this book is to show you how to become one of them. Once you master this skill, you will be doing what's best for yourself and for everyone around you.

That's the broad overview. When we begin to look more closely at assertiveness, however, the picture becomes more complex and even paradoxical. It's much easier to see what assertive *isn't* than what it *is*. While it's easy to characterize people who are blatantly aggressive or extremely passive, it's not always simple to express exactly what constitutes assertive behavior. This isn't really an unusual situation when talking about people's behavior. Like many other important human qualities, assertiveness is easier to recognize than it is to define. So let's look at the evidence. We'll begin by looking at some real-life situations in which the quality of assertiveness can come into play.

A REAL-LIFE EXAMPLE OF EFFECTIVE ASSERTIVENESS

Imagine that you've just completed an important project at work that consumed several weeks of your time. What a relief! The project involved working together with a large number of other people, and in the end it all went quite well despite the many different personalities involved. Everyone made a contribution, and the result was very successful. But the story doesn't end there. Now you find out, unfortunately, that one member of the team has been singled out for special praise by your supervisor. This seems totally arbitrary and unfair. For some reason, only this one person was called into the supervisor's office to receive a personal congratulation.

How would you feel when you heard about this? Not good, obviously. But more important, how would you respond? Would you respond at all? An aggressive person, of course, would feel hostility toward the manager and to the person who was singled out for praise. There would be angry feelings, and there might also be harsh words at some point. A passive person, on the other hand, would probably refuse to admit that anything questionable had taken place, and would certainly not take any action.

The assertive response is somewhere between those two extremes. To see what this involves, we have to begin with a principle that will influence all of the lessons throughout this book. Our focus here will be primarily on assertiveness and people skills in a business setting. We must, therefore, consistently have a professional viewpoint, as opposed to a personal one. In the situation we've just described, an assertive response involves knowing how you really feel and then finding a way to express those feelings in the context of a business environment.

Suppose, for example, you make an appointment with the manager in question to air your feelings. Even if you're personally hurt by the fact that someone else seems to be getting too much credit for the work your whole group performed, it would be a mistake to start by bringing those personal feelings into the discussion. This is a business setting, so keep the focus on business. No matter what you may think, it's going to sound like you're whining if you talk only about your personal feelings. "If you say something like, "I did just as much work as George, and now he's getting all the credit," you'll sound very unprofessional.

A more assertive approach would sound something like this: "I understand that you're pleased with George's work on the project, and I'm really glad to hear that, because he made some important contributions. There is one thing that concerns me. This was a group effort, and all of us devoted a significant amount of time to the project, including me. When the time comes for my performance review, I want to be sure that I receive the same recognition that George does. This is really important to me. While it would be gratifying, of course, if each of us could also receive a personal thank-you, my main concern is how this will affect my career opportunities in the organization."

By focusing on the business-related aspects of this situation, as opposed to the emotional elements, a very useful effect is created. It's one that we'll refer to a number of times in the book. You see, both the overly passive response and the overly aggressive one are essentially childlike behaviors. In any business setting, the person who seems most mature always comes out best. If you pout and whine or throw a tantrum, you'll be on the losing end of the encounter. You would do best by displaying assertiveness. It is the adult response between the two poles of childish acting-out.

If we look more closely at some specific components of assertive action, you'll begin to see how this idea of the child and the adult plays out.

BREAKING DOWN THE COMPONENTS OF ASSERTIVENESS

Assertiveness is an antidote to fear, shyness, passivity, and even anger, all of which are childlike emotions. Assertiveness means speaking up, making reasonable requests, and generally insisting that your rights be respected as a significant, equal human beings. Assertiveness is also the ability to express negative emotions without personalizing the problem. An assertive person knows how to question, to disagree, and even to refuse without seeming childish. Assertiveness is being able to question authority from a positive perspective. It's the power to ask Why?—not just to rebel but in order to assume responsibility for making things better.

For the balance of this chapter, we'll look at four specific steps we can follow to implement assertiveness in virtually any setting. These three steps will be the foundation of all the assertive strategies we'll be discussing in the first two chapters.

STEP 1: *Preparing with Self-Reflection*

Today there are a variety of assessment tools to help us determine our strength sand opportunities for improvement. Particularly useful are 360-degree assessments because input is received from a variety of sources and can help reveal our blind spots. Dale Carnegie Training offers a variety of assessment tools that can be found on their website, www.dalecarnegie.com/assessments.

For the purposes of this book, we will take an informal assessment as a first step toward becoming an assertive person and building assertiveness into your people skills repertoire. Once we recognize where we are right now, we can then recognize where changes are needed and believe in our ability to make those changes.

For example, are you a person who often feels that you're being taken advantage of? If so, ask yourself if this is really an accurate picture of what's happening in your life. If you decide that it is accurate, what needs to change? Chances are, you're someone who has difficulty saying no, even when "no" is exactly what's called for. It may be helpful to start writing down situations in which you've confronted this issue. Keep a diary of the times you've said no, including how you felt when you said it. If you do this for a period of time, you'll see how your inhibitions will diminish as you really begin to confront them.

Perhaps you're on the other end of the spectrum. Can you cite instances in which you've been very outspoken? Have any of these crossed the line into aggressive behavior? Be honest with yourself about this. If the answer is yes, ask yourself if this is really helping you or hurting you. Is aggressiveness something that you really want to build into your personality, or is it just a substitute for the more adult response that assertiveness represents? Once again, try keeping a log of situations in which you felt yourself becoming aggressive. Track your progress in gaining control over those feelings.

As you do this, be aware that positive change isn't going to happen by itself. You may feel some anxiety, or even real fear, about becoming an assertive person. Write about this in your diary. Is there someone you can talk with about the changes you're trying to make? Speak with that person about the specific situations and feelings that concern you.

You might also want to explore the origins of the emotions that you're feeling.

Where do your values in dealing with other people really come from? When you make a decision about how to behave in a specific situation, whose voice do you hear in your mind? Who are the people from the past who are subconsciously influencing your behavior in the present?

The truth is, as children we're bombarded with rules—don't be selfish, don't insist on being first, don't make mistakes, don't be emotional, don't be unreasonable, don't interrupt, and many more. Most of these rules are very valuable and well intentioned, but if they were downloaded into your consciousness with too much force, you may have magnified them beyond their original purpose. What's more, despite the good reasons for many of these rules, every one of them can legitimately be broken under certain conditions.

For example, you have a right to be first, at least sometimes. You are allowed to make mistakes, as long as you intend to learn from them. You have a right to say you don't have enough time for something, if in fact you really don't have enough time.

STEP 2: *Conducting an Honest Self-assessment*

Most feelings of submissiveness or aggressiveness have their roots in early life. It's time to identify those origins and to realize that you've outgrown them.

As this process of recognition takes place, be aware also of the harm that's done when you back away from appropriately assertive behavior. When you act aggressively, for example, you're likely to incur feelings of guilt that can become very burdensome over time. When you allow people or circumstances to dominate your legitimate needs, a loss of self-respect takes place. At first you may think that not trying to assert yourself is a choice, but eventually it can translate into a belief that you really don't have any power.

In any personal or professional development effort, accurate self-assessment is the essential first step, and you should pull out all the stops to do this successfully. It's not always easy to look in the mirror and really know what you're seeing, however, and it's certainly not easy for other people to tell you. Self-awareness and self-assessment are so crucial that taking a bold step in that direction is necessary and encouraged. Having someone you can talk with about your work toward becoming an assertive person is a critical element of self-assessment. There's a way in which that person can really help you with only a minimal effort on their part. Of course, you should make it clear that you'll return the favor if and when you're called upon to do so. Here's what's involved. Write an email to your friend in which you list a number of personality characteristics. Include traits that you think you already have, as well as others that are both negative and positive. For example, you may think of yourself as a humorous person or as a very conscientious individual. Write those down at the top of your list. Then think of attributes that you'd like to have. Maybe you'd like to be known as a very happy person, or as someone who's charitable or compassionate. Put those words in your list. Finally, include some undesirable qualities, such as "angry" or "insensitive."

When you email this list to your friend, include a number of email addresses to which your friend can forward the list. Attach a brief note in which you ask the addressees to check off the qualities on the list that seem to describe you. Assure them that when they return the list to your friend, he or she will send you the results with total anonymity assured.

When you get the results, you will probably be amazed by some of the things that people see in you that you've never seen in yourself. This is a great way to get honest feedback on who you are compared to who you think you are. It may take a little courage on your part to send out a list like this, but just doing so is an act of assertiveness in its own right. So give it a try.

STEP 3: *Assessing Your Outer World*

Once you've made some real effort toward self-assessment, it's time to turn your focus from the inside to the outside. In other words, assess the things that are going on in your life right now, especially in your working life. What specific situations are you involved with right now that will have a bearing on your career success? How are you dealing with those situations? Are you being too passive? Perhaps you're being overly aggressive?

Pick a specific circumstance that presently concerns you, and create an accurate overview of that situation. Then start making a specific, detailed plan about how to act assertively in that setting, based on the following guidelines.

First, if you were to speak directly to the other people involved in the situation, how would you describe both the situation itself and your feelings about it? You can write down this conversation, or you might want to literally act it out for your own benefit. Be very specific about what happened in the past, what's happening now, and what you'd like to see happen in the future. Don't make general accusations like "you're always hostile . . . you're always upset . . . you never take the time to communicate with me." Instead, use "I" and "it" statements, stick to the facts, and maintain emotional control.

Most important, don't enlarge the scope of the conversation beyond the circumstance you're now dealing with. It's all right to speak about the past, but only as it pertains to this particular situation. For example, you may want to say something about a discussion you had when you got started on this particular project, but don't talk about something that was said last month or last year in a completely different context. Be objective. Focus on what actually happened and what actually is happening. Don't get into issues of motivation or psychology. You only know what took place on the physical level. You can speculate about why that might have taken place, but now is not the time to do so.

If you do feel the need to talk about emotions, make sure they're your own. Use "I" statements, which show you take responsibility for your feelings. Try to focus on positive feelings related to your legitimate wants and needs, not on your resentment of another person. Describe the changes you'd like to see made. Be specific about things that you'd like to see stop, as well as things that you'd like to see start. Be sure the requested changes are reasonable. Assertiveness includes consideration of other people's needs too, along with being willing to make changes in yourself in return. You may want to speak about the consequences of change or the absence of change, but don't make threats. Threats always personalize a conflict situation. They challenge people on a deeper level than a professional situation encompasses, and that can cause someone to feel cornered and defiant.

As you create these imaginary dialogues, start your sentences with phrases like these:

"What we might do is . . ."

"We could do . . ."

"Would you . . .?"

"I appreciate it when you . . ."

"I agree with some of what you're saying, and here's what I would like to see changed. . . ."

When you've had some practice in making up your scenarios of assertiveness, certain things will become clear to you. You'll begin to realize a few undeniable facts. You'll realize that no matter how calm and tactful you are, or how much you use "I" and "it" statements, or how much you stick to the specific situation, there will still be times when your assertiveness will be perceived as a personal assault. This perception may have no basis in reality. If the other individual happens to be an aggressive person, you may find yourself receiving just the kind of attack you're being accused of perpetrating. In order to be a really assertive person, you have to be prepared for this and know how to respond.

How to Respond to Aggression

Most of the time, simply explaining your position and standing your ground will handle the situation. You may, however, also have a strong temptation either to counterattack or to retreat. Try to resist both of these temptations. When the other person raises the stakes of the dialogue by becoming emotional, don't let that influence your behavior.

What's really happening is this: By becoming angry, the other party is implying that his or her feelings are more important than yours simply because he or she is speaking loudly or being sarcastic or even bursting into tears. Don't let that behavior diminish your own importance or elevate that of the other person. Don't respond with aggressiveness of your own. By the same token, don't simply back off. This is simply a passive-aggressive approach.

Instead, maintain an attitude that says "we both count equally." Dale Carnegie says we benefit most when we try to see things from the other person's point of view. This may not be easy if the other person starts to get emotional. Maintaining this attitude takes practice. Once again, there's a role for a close friend or a colleague here. Ask someone to role-play the conversation with you so that you can focus on keeping your poise.

This doesn't mean you should be dishonest just in order to hold your ground. If some of the criticism that you're getting is justified, acknowledge that the criticism is true. Don't make excuses. Even if you don't agree with most of the criticism, you can single out some part that you do agree with in order to lower the temperature of the discussion. Use phrases like "You could be right about that. . . ." or "I understand how you feel. . . ." Under other circumstances this may seem like you're backing down, but there are also times when some conciliation can be a good approach.

Remember, so far we've only been talking about how to practice and prepare for encounters in the real world. We've suggested that you keep a diary of aggressive and passive behavior on your part. We've talked about some self-assessment techniques, and we've suggested some role-playing exercises you can do with a friend. Now you're ready to "road-test" what you've been practicing.

STEP 4: *Taking the Road Test*

As you begin to test your assertiveness in real-life situations, here are some guidelines to keep in mind. First, pick a manageable set of circumstances. Start with easier, less stressful situations. Build some confidence. As you become more comfortable, you can make adjustments in your approach and prepare for more difficult situations.

If there isn't a situation in your life right now that seems to demand assertiveness, see if you can devise one. It's just a matter of stepping slightly outside your comfort zone. If you're in a meeting, ask a question or tactfully challenge someone to explain a point. Write a note or an email to a senior manager about something that concerns you. Offer a compliment or constructive feedback in a situation where you would normally have kept quiet. Don't do anything of a high-risk nature. It's just a matter of consciously becoming slightly and increasingly more assertive. Pay attention to how this intentional shift makes you feel. As always, writing can help to clarify your thoughts, so try putting some of this down in your assertiveness diary.

As your confidence grows, you'll be ready to take on more challenging situations. Over a period of a week or two, make a list of settings in which you'd like to assert yourself more strongly. Watch how these situations develop for a while before you take any action. Then pick one and decide what form truly assertive behavior would take in that setting. In other words, what is the best way to communicate your legitimate ideas, wants, and needs? Also, what is the best way to identify and eliminate wrongful behavior by the other parties? Finally, take action based on these insights.

Here are a couple of useful thoughts to bear in mind as you do this. Although some conversations may seem to be one-sided, most business interactions consist of two or more people disclosing their thoughts, feelings, or wishes, and trying to get their way. So, as you assertively express yourself, give the other party a chance to do the same, as you listen empathetically. Recognize that a win for you and a defeat for the other person is not the ideal outcome. An all-win, or at least the perception of one, is the target to be aiming for. In many situations it may take time to work this out. Sometimes you will be justified in demanding an immediate redress of grievances, while at other times this would be counterproductive. Under all circumstances, however, remember that assertiveness is really the modern equivalent of the Golden Rule. Honor the wants and needs of others, and expect that they will do the same for you. Don't settle for anything less.

ACTION STEPS

1. Reflect on an "unfair" incident in which you were involved, either in your workplace or in your personal life. How did you handle it? Write about the experience and then reflect on how you might handle it differently given the new concepts you have just learned.

2. Conduct an honest assessment of yourself. On a scale of 1 to 10, how assertive are you?

1   2   3   4   5   6   7   8   9   10

Passive   *Assertive*   *Aggressive*

3. Go through the list below and mark an X beside any trait that you currently have and would like to shift. Then write out an action plan to do so.

    ☐   I often feel I'm a victim of circumstances around me.

    ☐   I lash out at others when I am upset or feeling unfairly treated.

    ☐   I often open communications with "you make me . . ."

☐   I have a difficult time admitting that I am wrong.

☐   I overburden myself and don't say no often enough.

☐   I am overcritical of others and myself.

☐   I often use the illogical and extreme terms "never" and "always" when talking to another about his or her behavior.

☐   I avoid confrontation at all costs and shy away from being assertive.

ACTION PLAN NOTES

Make the other person happy about doing the thing you suggest.

—Dale Carnegie

CHAPTER 2

The Three-Part Assertion Message

In the previous chapter we looked at what assertiveness really is and we discussed some ways of preparing to bring assertiveness into your life and career. In this chapter we'll look at specific tactics you can use for actually applying assertiveness in a variety of workplace situations.

There are many techniques for implementing assertive behavior, but most are based on what can be called the three-part assertion message:

1. Summarize the facts of the situation.

2. Express your thoughts and feelings.

3. Clearly state your wants and needs, including benefits to the other party.

This three-part formula lets you express your concerns without being personally aggressive. The formula is simple, but using it can take practice and self-control. Let's look at an example of how the formula might play out in an actual conversation between two people in a business setting.

Nicole is the owner of a website design company. Her clients often need to have the content of their websites changed on short notice. As new products or services become available, the clients want that information put online as soon as possible for the benefit of potential customers.

Recently Nicole has become concerned that one of her designers has not met the agreed-upon deadlines for completing projects. Needless to say, this has created some displeasure among Nicole's clients, so she decides to speak with the designer about the situation.

Nicole will use the three-part assertion message formula. She begins by clearly and directly stating the facts. She says, "I recall our speaking about how long it would take you to turn around the work on this website assignment. We agreed that the whole job would take ten working days. It's been two weeks and the job isn't finished."

Notice that Nicole has not referred to anything except objective facts. She hasn't said anything about her worries or feelings. That all comes in the second part of the three-part assertion message.

"When there are delays like this," Nicole continues, "it creates tension for the client, and that translates into stress for us. I get concerned, and I have to communicate that concern to you."

With the third part of the formula, Nicole clarifies the changes that need to be made. She says, "I want to make it very clear that when we set a deadline for a piece of work, that deadline has to be met. When we've talked about how long you'll need for an assignment, I think you may have been setting unrealistic deadlines for yourself. Maybe you've done that because you think it will give me the impression that you're a really fast worker. But that's not what I'm going to be thinking about if the deadline is impossible to meet."

So far Nicole has been speaking only about the problem that needs to be solved, and how solving that problem will benefit her and her company. But remember, in any assertive dialogue it's important to include benefits for the person you're speaking with, if at all possible.

So here's how Nicole does this. She says, "In the future, when we talk about how long you'll need for an assignment, it will be much better to give yourself a little more time than you think you'll need, rather than less. I'm sure that will make your life easier and less stressful. When you complete the work on time, the client will be happy and so will I. And if you should happen to get the work done in less time than you've asked for, everyone will be pleasantly surprised."

In Nicole's example you can see the differences between assertiveness and aggression. Even when Nicole talks about her feelings, the only feelings she mentions are work-related. She doesn't say, "You're deliberately trying to annoy me," or "I'm really angry about this." If she had said anything like that, it would have opened the door for the employee to start verbalizing his or her own emotional responses, or at least to start thinking about them. This could quickly have taken the whole conversation way off course.

There's another aspect of this imaginary dialogue that's very important. Notice that the person who is being assertive here is the manager, not the subordinate. In thinking about assertiveness, we might assume that the person who needs this tool will always be the underdog. But supervisors need to be assertive too. Assertiveness is not really about power. It's about self-respect. It's about standing up for what you believe in and what you want, based on who you are as a human being and as a participant in a business operation. Since managers have this right just as much as anyone else, assertiveness skills are essential.

A MORE DETAILED LOOK AT ASSERTIVENESS TACTICS

The three-part assertion message is an excellent basic formula for business communication. But it would be simplistic to say that this is all you need to know about assertiveness tactics. With the three-part formula as a foundation, let's look in more detail at assertiveness tactics.

What happens, for example, if you encounter some resistance on the part of the person you're speaking with? In the dialogue we just presented, what should Nicole have done if her employee disagreed with her or even aggressively disagreed with her?

The truth is that some people just don't like to hear feedback and tend to take feedback personally. They see things a certain way, and they resist change. If anybody's going to make changes, they want it to be you. But an assertive person knows how to deal with that. If you're dealing with an inflexible individual, a good tactic is a little inflexibility on your own part.

This means calmly, firmly, and clearly stating your needs. If Nicole's employee says, "I didn't create an unrealistically short deadline," Nicole should say, "While the deadline may not have seemed unrealistic, the work is not complete. In the future, I want you to give yourself more time." If the employee says, "Tell the client to calm down," Nicole should say, "The best way to calm down the customer is by providing the work we promised on time. In the future, it would be wise to give yourself more time." It's just a matter of repeating the same statement in exactly the same way until the other person gets the message (regardless of any excuses, diversions, or arguments). Keep calm and stick to the point. Always respect the rights of the other person. And always ask yourself these questions:

- How can I express my message more clearly?

- How can I be more specific about what I have to say?

- How can I avoid being drawn off course by the other person?

Like most people, you may sometimes have felt a sense of remorse following a moment when you should have taken an assertive stand but didn't. And you've probably replayed that scenario in your head many times, with a better but imaginary outcome. This mental exercise may provide you with some brief satisfaction—at least until the same thing happens again.

There are plenty of instances in life, both minor and major, when we could use more assertiveness to stand up for ourselves. I'm sure you can think of many examples, complete with "this is what I should've done" variations. So, instead of fantasizing, let's look at some actual steps you can take the next time the need for assertiveness comes into your life.

Control your body language. When you're being berated or insulted, it is very easy to let your body speak for you instead of your mouth; you might fidget or nod, shrug your shoulders, or even offer an apologetic smile. All of these things are signs of conciliation, indicators that you are on the way to giving up. They weaken your position before you've even had a chance to start strengthening it.

More specifically, your first step should be limiting your *body language* to the greatest extent possible. Instead, stand or sit still and look the other person in the eye. Wait until they're done before you respond to anything that's said. Don't even bother trying to interrupt. This is their opportunity to let you have it, so give them that opportunity. Just make certain that when your chance to respond comes, you insist that nobody interrupts you. Whether you're dealing with a manager in a work situation or with someone regarding a personal matter, let them say their piece, then make it clear that you also deserve to be heard.

Speak in active, first-person terms. Stand up for yourself by keeping your language direct. Speak from your own point of view. Begin any response by grounding your sentences in the first person. Say, "I appreciate your point of view. . . . Have you considered . . . ?" Or, "I prefer to do it this—or not to do this—because . . ."

Or, "I think . . ." These phrases help you to stay grounded in the topic and also prevent you from launching personal attacks on others. Assertiveness isn't a debate contest, and it isn't a battle in which the best defense might be a good offense. This is defending your actions, motives, or opinions against frivolous attacks by others who seek to minimize you.

While the words *I'm sorry* might seem to apply, actually they do not. This is an expression of passivity, and you do not want to be in any way passive while trying to stand up for yourself. The same does not apply if you find that you have made a mistake. We should admit any mistake quickly and emphatically. However, never apologize for standing up for yourself; you can *apologize* later for saying something in the heat of the moment that wasn't especially wise (this is to be avoided with your boss) but never for defending yourself.

Bring the situation to a close. Someone else got this ball rolling by making you feel small. Take control of the situation by being the one to conclude it. If this means you need to stand up for yourself by offering an *ultimatum* and you can afford to do so, bring it on. You may also consider simply accepting the situation and saying, "I feel very strongly about this, so why don't we agree to disagree and move on?"

Most people who try to belittle others neither expect resistance nor know what to do when confronted with it. Faced with their unknown and possibly unreliable reaction, shut down the situation before you have to find out what it might be. Reassert your position, if necessary, so that you're coming across as someone who believes in himself and his talents. To accomplish this, you might suggest a solution or, if you can live with it, a compromise. Look hard for the former, and don't be too eager for the latter!

DALE CARNEGIE'S INSIGHTS

On the subject of assertiveness tactics, it's interesting and even inspiring to realize how much Dale Carnegie understood about this as early as the 1930s! To this day, there has never been a better strategist and tactician of assertiveness than Dale Carnegie. He may not have used that exact word, but he had a deep understanding of assertiveness and how to put it into action. The best proof of this comes from simply looking at what Dale Carnegie actually had to say.

Interviewing Assertively

An important recurring experience in every adult's life is the interview for some much-desired objective. The interview may be for a job, or for a loan, or for a chance to have your student film entered in a festival or competition. These interviews can be important turning points, even on the scale of your whole life, so you'll want them to go as well as possible. In fact, it's fair to say you need them to go as well as possible. So let's see exactly what you can do toward that end.

Be prepared. *Of all the interview tips we could possibly discuss, "preparation" is the most important word and the most important part of the whole process. With good preparation, everything will go as planned and you will get the result you desire. Without preparation, that result is impossible—partly because it's not even clear in our own minds what the result should be. As the saying goes, if you don't know where you're going, you will never get there.*

Before taking part in any interview, do some research so that you know some basic information about the person or persons you will be meeting. If you're interviewing for a job, what kind of company will you be working for? What is its history? Who were its founders? What is its mission statement? How does that statement express itself in the company's way of doing business in the real world? This information will provide you with a foundation to intelligently answer the questions that will come up during the actual interview session.

Your research should include specific job-related issues and requirements. You definitely don't want to be faced with some tricky question asked by the interviewer, which catches you totally off guard. The only reason that could possibly happen is that you've simply dropped the ball regarding preparation.

Here's a good technique: Look at yourself in the mirror! What could be simpler? Go through the procedure of "interviewing yourself," with special attention to weak points in your appearance, your body language, and your knowledge of the relevant issues. Portraying confidence and assertiveness are surely the most important parts of an interview. Every interviewer will want to see that you're sure of yourself, and that your high confidence is a reflection of your true abilities.

Look the part. *Using the same concept as when preparing a résumé, your appearance will play a key role in presenting a good image of yourself. We wouldn't expect an employer to be wearing running shoes and jeans, so why should we? Dress appropriately for the job at hand. Administrative and managerial jobs require a suit and tie for men and corresponding attire for women. Don't overdress, but it's better to be too formal than excessively casual.*

Winning tactics. *Here are the three simple, essential things to do when entering the interview site and meeting the person with whom you'll be talking:*

- *Introduce yourself by clearly stating your name.*

- *Make direct eye contact with the interviewer. Get a pleasant expression on your face!*

- *Give a firm handshake—a little firmer than you think it ought to be.*

On the flip side, here are some behaviors to avoid:

- *Sit up straight and don't slouch. Sitting up portrays confidence and energy.*

- *Keep still! Constantly moving your hands or feet will suggest nervousness.*

- *Think before you speak. Make a conscious decision to wait before you answer a question. Even one second is helpful when trying to collect and organize your thoughts.*

Unless you're interviewed by a very creative or eccentric person, certain questions are almost guaranteed to come up. Here are some of the most predictable categories.

Plain vanilla. Every job interview contains a series of questions tailored for that specific applicant. But most interviews actually comprise a set of generic questions that would come up in almost any situation, whether it is an interview for a prospective kindergarten teacher or for a graduate school professor.

Below is a list to give you an idea of the types of questions that might come up in conversation during an interview. The key is to answer the questions sincerely, thoughtfully, and with clarity.

- *What experience do you have for the position?*

- *Besides your experience, what makes you an outstanding candidate?*

- *Where do you see yourself five years in the future?*

- *Why do you want to work for our company in particular?*

- *What specific skills can you bring to our company?*

Take the appropriate time to answer each one of the questions. Again, it's important to seem confident without giving the impression that you think the position is already yours. Interviewers always pick up on this, and a sense of complacency could work

*against you during the hiring process. Give your best effort during
the entire interview until the very end.*

*There are different levels of interviews, from the preliminary
one to the final selection. Each stage will offer different levels of
difficulty and require different preparation. But with the basic
knowledge, you should be ready to face any interview situation.*

STARTING MEETINGS ON A POSITIVE NOTE

In most business discussions, a prerequisite for success is
assertiveness without aggressiveness by either party. To achieve
this, Dale Carnegie suggests beginning the conversation with
praise and honest appreciation. For what? For almost anything!
In short, start on a positive note. Before your meeting, think
carefully about the positive note on which you'll begin. There's
no need to turn this into a speech or formal statement. Just
mention something that will create a positive connection from the
outset. If you haven't had previous contact with the other party,
say something positive about the organization, about a colleague
whom you both know, about the local community, or almost
anything (with the possible exception of the weather). Ideally,
you'll be able to refer to some successful project in the past
that the two of you worked on together. Again, that's not really
necessary. The main thing is to say something that has a positive
tone. At the most basic level you could express appreciation for
having the meeting set up.

TAKE AN INDIRECT APPROACH

If the purpose of the meeting is to discuss a mistake or
disagreement, move toward this topic indirectly. This indirect
approach is another of Dale Carnegie's very insightful principles.
As Carnegie so well understood, it's a mistake to confuse being
assertive with being merely blunt or tactless. To simply come out
and accuse someone of wrongdoing or incompetence is almost

always a poor tactic. This just forces the other party into a defensive mode where very little can be accomplished.

As Mr. Carnegie suggested, it's a good idea to talk about your own mistakes before criticizing another person. When giving feedback, an assertive approach focuses on future solutions. Mistakes in the past should be seen as signposts pointing in the direction of better performance in the future. The emphasis should always be on objective experiences and criteria rather than on someone's internal shortcomings.

Imagine, for example, that a sales manager is having a talk with one of her reps. The manager is very concerned about the rep's recent performance. "Your productivity is way down lately," she says. "Why is this happening? What's the matter with you?"

From the rep's point of view, questions like that are very difficult to answer. The questions are far too open-ended and personal. They refer to who the rep is rather than what the rep has done or not done. "What's the matter with you?" raises issues that are best taken up in a psychotherapy session. It's not the kind of language that should come up in a business discussion.

For a much more productive approach, the manager might say something like this: "Last month you were one of our top producers. Lately things seem to have slowed down a little. I know how that can happen, because I've seen fluctuations like that in my own work. Can you think of anything that might have caused this change?"

Here the emphasis is on what actually happened rather than on the deep underlying issues. Notice also that the manager creates empathy with the rep by referring to her own similar experiences. This is not weakness on the manager's part. It's assertive behavior in the best sense of the word.

QUESTIONING OVER ORDERING

As another tactic of assertiveness, Dale Carnegie stressed the benefits of asking questions rather than giving direct orders. If a manager says to a rep, "I want to see a list of all the calls you make before noon every day," the rep's defenses are understandably going to go up. Whenever an adult is spoken to like a child, there will be resistance.

A more genuinely assertive tactic by the manager would sound something like this: "In my own work, I've noticed that good time management is closely tied with productivity. When I keep track of how I'm using my time, I tend to get much better results. Have you ever tried keeping a log of how you use your time? Why don't you try that for a couple of days? If you want, we can look over it together and see what it tells us."

This is real assertiveness in action. There's an implied reprimand that's surrounded by empathy and encouragement. While an aggressive approach makes the problem seem deep and mysterious, assertive dialogue puts it on the surface, where it seems easy to correct. Instead of feeling threatened, people will feel happy about doing the things you suggest.

While it's hard to do anything but agree when suggestions are put this way, the process isn't over. Whenever constructive direction has been given, be sure to follow it up with praise for any improvement, no matter how slight. In this way, a person who might otherwise feel diminished by criticism acquires a fine reputation to live up to.

ENDING ON A POSITIVE NOTE

Dale Carnegie made all of these points very clear in his pioneering work on interpersonal behavior and relationships. He had one more insight that's often overlooked by people who confuse assertive tactics with aggressive behavior. Whenever you have to focus on a negative situation or deliver criticism of any kind, what happens at the close of the conversation is extremely important. Don't ever allow the discussion to end on a negative note. Don't let the other person walk away feeling put upon or victimized. Surprisingly, this is especially true when your criticism is very well justified, because that's when someone can feel very guilty and downhearted. Always give people the opportunity to save face. Always allow them an honorable retreat. This opens up the opportunity for a fresh start during your next interaction. Ending on a negative note leaves a lingering sense of negativity—and an assertive conversation, above all, should be a positive experience for everyone.

LOOKING AT REACTIONS

During these first two chapters, we've defined assertiveness and distinguished it from aggression and passivity. We've spoken about how to develop assertiveness from a strategic point of view through understanding the issues involved and through exercises you can do before taking assertive action in the everyday world. In this second chapter, we've been looking at tactical applications of assertiveness in contemporary business situations, and we've seen how Dale Carnegie anticipated those situations even in his earliest work. Before moving on to the sharply focused topics on assertiveness that will comprise our following chapters, let's look at some of the reactions you may get when you make assertiveness the basis for your business communications. Knowing how to recognize and deal with these reactions is extremely important. Unless you handle them correctly, you may indeed have behaved assertively while you were in the presence of the other party, and you won't get the action you desire after the conversation is completed.

By far the most common negative response to assertiveness is simple aggression by the other person. In some situations there may be raised voices, red faces, and fists pounded on the table, along with all kinds of threats and intimidation. The challenge here is to avoid being drawn into those kinds of behaviors. Assert your right to remain apart from them. If you've done your strategic work before the conversation took place, you can be sure you're in the right. So there's no need to apologize or back down. You can certainly express regret that the other person is upset. Having said that, you should then reaffirm your position. One of the most dangerous things about anger is the fact that it's so highly contagious. You need to create immunity from other people's anger by being aware of just how "catching" it can be.

And remember, even if people don't get angry in your presence during an assertive conversation, it's a mistake to let them leave before any harsh feelings are resolved. Otherwise you may find them expressing their anger about you to other people in the workplace instead of to your face. That can be even more difficult to deal with and can hurt morale.

Through the grapevine, you may hear that there has been complaining and grumbling around the water cooler. At least initially, the best tactic is to ignore this fallout. If it continues, you'll want to have another conversation in which you apply the same principles of assertiveness that we've been discussing. This time, however, make sure that any negative feelings come to the surface before you part ways, no matter how much anger that may include on the other person's part. As we've discussed, the challenge for you is to avoid being drawn into the anger.

Whether in your presence or behind your back, overtly aggressive behavior is actually easier to deal with than passive-aggressive responses to an assertive conversation. Pouting, self-pity, excuse making, and even crying are very common. Once again, be sympathetic without backing down. Simply repeat your core message quietly but firmly, no matter how much drama you may encounter.

Some individuals react to assertiveness by taunting, trying to undermine your argument and position, and other such behavior. It is important to deal with those reactions immediately, by pointing out what the person is doing and by affirming your position. If there are other people present, it's best to take the person aside rather than dealing with the problem publicly.

DEALING WITH DENIAL

It's also possible that an individual may deny everything you've been saying. You may be accused of completely fabricating a problem where none actually exists. This can be difficult, because you're talking about two opposing interpretations of reality. The other person may sincerely believe that you're completely mistaken. Here it's appropriate to apologize, in a hypothetical way, for any possible error on your part. Your response should probably sound something like this: "I've told you how things looked to me. I can understand if this is different from how things look to you. Based on my perceptions, I need to stand by what I said."

If the issue you've been discussing was sensitive enough, you may even encounter someone who complains of a health-related symptom. They may feel faint, for example, or complain of shortness of breath, or a sudden headache. This doesn't happen often, but when you're really asking people to change their behavior, you should be prepared for surprises of all kinds. There's no doubt, however, that in today's workplace you must take any physical complaints very seriously, especially if you're in a managerial position. The legal issues are so delicate that you must offer medical assistance whenever anyone mentions a physical problem. While there may not be anything seriously wrong, there's always the chance that something really is. In any case, you'll be protecting yourself from possible legal action.

So far we've talked about people who defend themselves against your assertive interventions. That defense may take the form of direct aggression against you, subversive behavior behind your back, or passive-aggressive acting out. On the other end of the spectrum, there are people who not only seem to agree with you but who can't seem to stop apologizing. This can be a very effective form of interpersonal jujitsu. Unless you know how to deal with it, such behavior can be challenging. The best response is to say quietly that apologies are not really necessary (or at least not more than once). Then reassert the appropriateness and fairness of what you've already said.

If you keep these tactical responses in mind, you'll find that your assertive behavior will bring you the best possible results. Of course, others may find it surprising or even shocking at the outset, especially if you have not been known for asserting yourself in the past.

There are several reasons why assertive behavior is so hard for some people to accept. Although the situation is beginning to change, educational institutions have tended to encourage nonassertive behavior. Often assertiveness has been mistaken for aggressiveness, thereby associating actions that may have been very much in the right with antisocial or disruptive behavior. The truth is, if you've had a conventional upbringing anytime over the last fifty years, you probably haven't learned the skills and responses that constitute genuine assertiveness. These behaviors can be learned, and the effort is hugely worthwhile.

As your assertiveness skills develop, you will find that they tend to neutralize the anxieties many people experience in various business situations. By learning, practicing, and trying out assertive responses, you'll find that there's a marked reduction in stress of all kinds. In fact, learning appropriate assertive behavior is one of the main ways by which anxiety is now treated.

Learning to be more assertive, therefore, can lead to greater emotional freedom in general. People who are very nonassertive, passive, and inhibited often have difficulty freely expressing other emotions, like tenderness and real affection. Learning to express justified annoyance and anger and to assert one's rights in a firm and straightforward manner makes it easier to relate to people in a friendly and caring way.

One of the greatest benefits of learning assertiveness is the increase it will bring in your sense of freedom and self-respect. No one should be subject to the domination, whims, and aggression of others. There is only one way to eliminate those restrictions, and that's by being appropriately assertive with anyone who tries to dominate or stifle you, especially in business situations. People have to be free in choosing their actions. Right now, if you're unable to be assertive in a business situation, then you're not free. The information you'll get in the chapters that follow will change that forever.

PERFECT PRACTICE MAKES PERFECT

Very few people are aggressive nearly all the time and in all situations. Likewise, very few individuals are totally without assertiveness in all situations. More typically, people hold their own in some circumstances and are nonassertive in others. The task is to analyze these various settings and become more fully aware of how you respond in each of them. Observe, ask for advice and coaching, and learn alternative ways of acting. Once you learn the right way to respond, you can be assured that perfect practice will create perfection. First try your new approach in thought or in written exercises, and gradually in real-life situations.

As you learn more about assertiveness, it's important not to hurry the progression from exercises to application in the workplace. Take your time. Sometimes there's a temptation to progress too quickly. Recognize that there will be some ups and downs in the learning curve. Although the reactions of others to assertiveness are usually quite positive, as we discussed earlier, some people respond in an adverse way. Just remember these basic facts: It is your right to stand up for yourself and to assert your individuality. On the other hand, you don't have to be assertive all the time, in all circumstances. The goal is to have the power to assert yourself, and to be free to make that choice.

In closing, here are some questions to keep in mind that will help you to keep track of your assertiveness. When you first read these questions, you may want to just answer yes or no. When you read these questions again, try to compare your progress with how you felt in the past. Then set a goal for where you want to be next time.

- ☐ When you differ with someone you respect, are you able to speak up and share your own viewpoint?

- ☐ Are you able to refuse unreasonable requests made by your coworkers, and even by your supervisors?

- ☐ Do you readily accept positive criticism and suggestion?

- ☐ Do you ask for assistance when you need it?

- ☐ Do you always have confidence in your own judgment?

- ☐ If someone else has a better solution to a problem than what you had thought of, do you accept it gracefully?

- ☐ Do you express your thoughts, feelings, and beliefs in a direct and honest way?

- ☐ Do you try to work for an all-win solution that benefits all parties?

If you answered yes to the majority of these questions, you're well on your way to an assertive approach to life and your career. The topics in the chapters that follow will very quickly take you to the next level of mastery. If you didn't answer yes, you're reading the right book! Please continue reading. You'll gain much-needed and valuable insights.

ACTION STEPS

1. Dale Carnegie suggested that you always start with referencing mistakes that you've made before criticizing others. Are you able to do so? If not, how might you shift your self-perception in order to have the confidence to admit your errors?

2. Reflect on your communication skills. Do you ever order others as opposed to asking questions? If so, when? What steps can you take to change your communication style?

3. Do you ever succumb to intimidation? If so, with whom? What small steps can you take to stand firmer in your convictions?

4. Make a list of those things that you most value and respect about yourself. Then make a list of those attributes that need work. Take some time to honor yourself for your positive attributes. Also take the time to honor yourself for recognizing and working on those attributes that do not best serve you.

ACTION PLAN NOTES

Begin with praise and honest appreciation.

—Dale Carnegie

CHAPTER 3

Assertive Rapport Building

I n the previous two chapters, we looked at strategies of assertive behavior and how to plan and prepare for encounters in which you'll act assertively. Then we spoke about approaches that you can put into action when you're face-to-face with another person or a group. Now, and in the rest of the book, we'll focus on using assertiveness to attain specific results in your dealings with other people. In this chapter we will focus on the first of the essential people skills, assertive rapport building. We will see what it takes to connect with another individual. We'll be looking at two elements in particular: self-confidence and the ability to build interpersonal rapport.

ASSERTIVENESS AND SELF-CONFIDENCE

Building self-confidence and assertiveness is probably a lot easier than you think. Most "nonassertive" people don't want to transform into excessively dominant individuals. When most people talk about being more assertive, what they really mean is:

- Becoming better able to resist the pressure and dominance of aggressive people

- Having the ability to stand up for their own beliefs

- Being able to maintain control in important situations

Pure assertiveness—dominance for the sake of being dominant—is not a desirable trait for most people. An aggressive, pushy personal style tends to be driven by some insecurity. Most people know this and it's not something they admire or want for themselves. Still, anyone seeking to increase their own assertiveness should understand the typical personality and motivation of excessively dominant people, who incidentally cause the most worry to nonassertive people.

It's essential also to understand the distinction between leadership and dominance. Real leadership is inclusive and proactive. It does not dominate nonassertive people. It includes them and it involves them. Dominance as a management style is ineffective in almost all circumstances. It is based on short-term rewards and results, mostly for the benefit of the dominant leader, and it fails completely to make effective use of what team members have to offer.

Bullies are a specific type of dominant people. Deep down, they are very insecure people. They dominate because they are too insecure to allow other people to have responsibility and influence, and this behavior is generally conditioned from childhood for one reason or another. The dominant bullying behavior is effectively reinforced by the response given by "secure" and "nonassertive" people to bullying. The bully gets his or her own way. The bullying dominant behavior is rewarded, and so it goes on.

On its own terms, bullying works—at least until it doesn't. Bullies are generally concerned with satisfying their need to get their own way, to control, to achieve status, to manipulate, make decisions, build empires, to collect material signs of achievement and wealth, and especially to establish a protective mechanism of "yes-men" followers. Early childhood experiences usually play an important part in creating bullies, who are victims as well as aggressors. Although it's a tough challenge for anyone on the receiving end of their behavior, bullies actually deserve sympathy.

Nonassertive people normally do not actually aspire to being excessively dominant people, and they certainly don't normally want to become bullies. When most people talk about wanting to be more assertive, what they really mean is "I'd like to be more able to resist the pressure and dominance of overly aggressive people." Doing this is not really so hard, and by using simple techniques, it can even be quite enjoyable and fulfilling.

Nonassertive people should understand where they really are starting from. Nonassertive behavior is often a sign of strength, not weakness—and it is the most appropriate choice for many situations. Don't make the mistake of thinking that you always have to be more and more assertive.

Understand where you want to be. What level of assertiveness do you want? Chances are, you're mostly interested in protecting and defending yourself and others, not in projecting your will onto the world.

For people who are not naturally assertive, it is possible to achieve a perfectly suitable level of change with a few simple techniques, rather than trying to transform yourself into a fundamentally different kind of person. Here are some user-friendly tools for developing self-confidence and more assertive behavior.

Know the facts relating to the situation and have them at hand. Do some research. Most overbearing people fail to prepare their facts; they try to dominate through bluster, reputation, and force of personality. If you know and can produce facts to support or defend your position, it is unlikely that the aggressor will have anything prepared in response. When you know that a situation is going to arise over which you'd like to have some influence, prepare your facts, do your research, do the math, get the facts and figures, solicit opinions and views, be able to quote sources. Then you will be able to make a firm case and also dramatically improve your reputation for being someone who is organized, firm, and appropriately assertive.

Anticipate other people's behavior and prepare your responses. Roleplay in your own mind how things are likely to happen. Prepare your responses according to the different scenarios that you think could unfold. Identify other people who may be present to support and defend you. Being well prepared will increase your self-confidence and enable you to be assertive about what's important to you.

Prepare effective questions of your own. Asking good questions is the most reliable way of gaining the initiative. Questions most disliked by dominating individuals are deep, constructive, incisive, and probing—especially if the question exposes a lack of thought, preparation, consideration, or consultation on their part. For example:

- What is your evidence (for what you have said or claimed)?

- Whom have you consulted about this?

- How did you go about looking for alternative solutions?

- How have you measured (whatever you say is a problem)?

- How will you measure the true effectiveness of your solution if you implement it?

- What can you say about different solutions that have worked in other situations?

And don't let yourself get brushed aside. Stick to your guns. If the question is avoided, return to it or rephrase it.

Recondition your reactions to dominant people. Try to visualize yourself behaving in a firm manner, armed with well-prepared facts and evidence. Practice saying things like "Hold on a minute—I need to consider what you have just said." Also practice saying "I'm not sure about that. It's too important to make a snap decision now." Don't cave in for fear that someone might shout at you or have a tantrum.

Have faith that your own abilities will work if you use them. Nonassertive people are often extremely strong in areas of process, detail, dependability, reliability, and working cooperatively with others. These capabilities all have the potential to undo a dominating personality who has no proper justification. Recognize your strengths and use them to defend and support your position.

BUILDING RAPPORT IS KEY

Developing a personal rapport will not only makes business dealings more fun but can also serve as the foundation for mutually beneficial interactions.

Rapport is not necessarily a word we use every day, but we've chosen it carefully here because it refers to something very specific that happens between people. Here's a dictionary definition of rapport: "an emotional bond or friendly relationship based on mutual liking and trust, and a sense that wants, needs, and concerns are mutually understood."

At the outset, let me call your attention to four words in the definition you've just read. The words are *mutual liking and trust.* Words like that don't often enter into discussions of business success or negotiating strategies. More frequently, we're used to hearing about power or intimidation. There may be a place for those qualities in the business world, but they don't come under the category of people skills.

Some of the rapport-building topics we'll cover in this chapter may seem obvious, but pay attention. You'd be surprised how many people set up interpersonal obstacles without even knowing it.

When a new person comes into your life, whether by chance meeting or formal introduction, how do you decide what you're going to say and do? Actually, for many people this isn't a decision at all. They just play it by ear. They present themselves to one person pretty much the way they've done with others. Their people skills in this respect are a matter of habit more than anything else.

Changing that is the first step toward assertive rapport building. Assertiveness is the opposite of passivity, and continuing to do what is comfortable can be a form of passivity. So, when you first meet someone, don't take anything for granted. Realize that new acquaintances may know nothing about you, and you should not assume that you know anything about them. Of prime importance is the understanding that people have diverse upbringings, backgrounds, and value systems. With a new person, therefore, be very careful about voicing any strong personal opinions you might have, especially of a negative nature. Ask open-ended questions, maintain eye contact, and be a good listener. Be positive in every respect and make a sincere attempt to discover shared values or common interests. Show that you're glad to meet this exciting new individual. And, most important . . . smile!

A SMILE GOES A LONG WAY

The positive effect of having a smile on your face may seem obvious, but smiling is so crucial to building rapport that we need to spend a moment focused on it. Literally from day one of a person's life, seeing a smiling human face elicits a hugely positive reaction. This is something that's hardwired into our consciousness. It's universal. It's eternal. So just do it!

It may surprise you to hear this, but as with other forms of assertive behavior, you should practice your smile. That's right, stand in front of a mirror and see how you look. Pay attention to your eyes. Are they congruent with your smile?

The amazing thing about smiling is the effect it will have on you as well as on anyone you meet. When the muscles of the face contract in a smile, the experience is reflected in the production of neurotransmitters in the brain. By looking and acting happy, you can literally make yourself feel happy. There's just no way to overstate the importance of smiling as a rapport-building action. It's probably the single best thing you can do to connect with others and have people drawn to you. People like to be around happy and energetic people.

While you're smiling at your new acquaintance, why not try to say something complimentary in a genuinely good-natured way? There's an art to doing this, and once again, you'll get better with practice. It doesn't have to be anything personal. If you're meeting someone in a new city, you might say something about what a good time you've been having. If it's the other party who's come to your hometown, say something of a welcoming nature. If you're greeting a new employee to your firm, make a sincere remark about how glad you are to have them aboard. If you're meeting with someone in their office, find something to praise on their wall or on their desk. You'll find the right thing to say once you really commit to saying something positive about the other person.

SPEAKING UP SPEAKS VOLUMES

As you're doing this, make sure that he or she can hear you. In other words, speak up. You don't have to yell, but be sure to speak clearly and articulate your words. The truth is, many people speak too softly and with too little energy or passion in their business conversations. There are many possible reasons for this. Maybe they don't want to come across as an overbearing personality. Maybe speaking in a quiet voice helps them to feel calm. Maybe they think this is a good way to prevent confrontations from developing. All those ideas make perfectly good sense, but are they real choices or are they just habits? Your normal vocal intonation is probably too soft. That may not matter too much in most situations, but be aware of your tendency. When you need to, be ready to change it assertively.

As an assertive person, you should know how to vary your voice quality to build rapport in different situations. You need to pay attention to volume, pace, and inflection. Once again, these should be conscious choices, not just habitual behaviors.

You should also pay attention to what you're saying as well as to how you say it. The fact is, the way you talk will determine the way you are perceived. What you say is often a reflection on how well you listen, and how you say it reflects upon your image. The ability to express yourself clearly, powerfully, diplomatically, and tactfully is essential to building rapport in an assertive way.

BE SPECIFIC WHEN ASSERTING YOUR IDEAS

As an extension of this, don't be afraid to stand up for your ideas, even if this causes some disagreement with others. Just be aware of the difference between being argumentative and being assertive. Differences of opinion are not a bad thing and can even be a healthy and positive growth experience, as long as they don't turn personal. The purpose of assertive disagreement is to find solutions to problems, solutions that both parties can agree on. That kind of winning scenario builds much better rapport than simply giving in to another person's opinion or forcing them to agree with yours.

When you're called upon to give praise or feedback, it's a good idea to think carefully about what you're going to say and to make your comments as specific and constructive as possible. This makes your praise more genuine, and it prevents criticism from sounding like a general indictment of someone's character. For example, it's better to say "I was really impressed with the way you handled that customer, by listening to her argument instead of interrupting" rather than to say "You're quite good with difficult people." The second comment is so general that it doesn't provide specific feedback about what was done well. In the same way, "In looking at our production schedule, I see that you missed the deadline for that report" is more effective than "Your time management skills are terrible." Again, the second statement is too general, subjective, and attacks the person.

Always follow praise or criticism with a word about the reasoning behind your comments. A good rule of thumb for giving people constructive criticism or feedback is to first check your motives and be sure you are not being manipulative. People need to know where you're coming from if you expect them to be motivated to action. For example, after you say, "You missed the deadline for the report," you might want to add, "Perhaps it's because you've been spending more time on telephone sales than we anticipated. Let's discuss how you can allocate your time in future."

In any case, never use positive or negative comments as a way of manipulating people into doing something for you. Don't try something like this: "You are the most hardworking member of the department and I really appreciate the effort you put in for the meeting this afternoon. Maybe you could write up the minutes for me?" Whether they let on or not, employees instantly see through that kind of tactic. It undercuts everything you've already said, and it makes whatever you might say in the future much more difficult to believe.

HOW TO SPEAK OF YOUR OWN ACCOMPLISHMENTS

As long as we're on the topic of how to build rapport through what we say about others, we should certainly look at the importance of what we say about ourselves. Assertive people know how to speak well of themselves without appearing boastful. There are many effective approaches for doing this. A great way to compliment yourself, for example, is by complimenting others first. If someone tells you he went to the University of Michigan and you say, "Wow, that's a great school," he's probably going to ask you where you went. That's when you can respond, "Harvard!" or "Slippery Rock!" or whatever the case may be. So a rapport-building objective has been achieved. You've made someone else feel good, and you've gotten to feel good in return.

When you're speaking about your own accomplishments, resist the temptation to embellish or dramatize the facts. Emphasize the hard work and effort that others put into helping you achieve the goal. If in fact you are the one who closed the big deal, you'll be recognized for your accomplishment, even if you give credit to others. In fact, you'll gain trust, credibility, and respect by sharing the glory.

CULTIVATING ASSERTIVE SILENCE

Since we've spent this much time on the subject of how to speak, we should also say something about the power of silence. Silence can be a great rapport-building tool. Just as what you say can help you develop rapport, what you don't say can also be of great benefit. Assertive and confident people understand that.

Without a doubt, you've been around people who seem to have a fear of silence. It's a dread of what might happen if every single second isn't filled up with speech of some kind. There may also be an element of not wanting to seem antisocial or unfriendly. But remaining silent occasionally isn't the same as refusing to participate in a conversation. Especially in a business setting, silence doesn't equate with anger or impulsively clamming up. Appropriate silence, assertive silence, means purposefully choosing to be quiet, listening with full attention, and making the decision not to speak unless you know the purpose for doing so.

Regarding the importance of silence, what you wear is one of the best ways of making a statement without words. Just as in other areas, there's a difference between looking too passive, looking too aggressive, and dressing with proper assertiveness. If you blend in with the business environment in which you are surrounded by wearing appropriate attire, building rapport tends to come more easily.

BEWARE OF LEAKS

There's a very interesting concept that pertains to all the topics we've been discussing in this chapter—how you speak, how you dress, whether you smile or have a gloomy look on your face. This concept is something that psychologists refer to as a leak. In terms of human interaction, a leak is a behavior that reveals something about a person that the person had been trying to keep hidden. Stealing a glance at your watch, for instance, is a leak. You may have been trying to give the impression that you were listening closely to what another person was saying, but if you look at your watch (and get caught at it), you've leaked the fact that you can't wait for the conversation to be over. A confident and assertive approach might be "I hate to cut our meeting short, but I have another meeting in just a few minutes."

THREE CHOICES

The way people behave toward one another can be categorized in three ways: passive, aggressive, and assertive. And the choice is always yours.

If you tend to act passively, then you may be seeking to avoid conflict, often at the expense of your own needs.

If you tend to act aggressively, you may go to the other extreme and escalate conflict in an attempt (not always successful) to get your own needs met.

Most people would agree that usually it is best to avoid both these extremes, if you can, and act assertively—it's best to express your own needs and wants, not hide them, but to do so in a way that is reasonable and that allows others the opportunity to communicate their wishes and feelings too.

If you are in a relationship or a work situation where you feel that your needs are not being met or that the other person is acting in a way you don't like, then it will usually be helpful to express your feelings and thoughts assertively rather than to conceal them passively or to express them too aggressively.

Following are some specific tips for preparing yourself before entering into a conversation, discussion, or negotiation with someone where you want to try to get the other person to act in a different way or treat you differently.

1. Write down in advance an outline of what you intend to say to the other person.

2. In the outline, describe the situation or behavior that is creating a problem for you and that you would like the person to change.

3. When describing the situation, be specific and give examples of when the behavior has occurred.

4. Avoid using exaggerations or generalizations. Be honest and keep your description as straightforward and simple as possible.

5. Express your thoughts and feelings about the situation, acknowledging them as your own thoughts and feelings rather than expressing them as a general truth.

6. Ask for reasonable changes from the other person that would help to improve the situation for you.

7. Listen to what the other person has to say in response—without necessarily agreeing with it.

8. If there is a "win-win" situation where a change in the other person's behavior—or yours—will benefit them as well as you, try to explore that possibility with them.

9. If there is no win-win situation, then decide beforehand on the minimum outcome you need. Be prepared to negotiate a solution between the minimum and the maximum that you would like.

10. Focus on areas where you might compromise. Think of suggestions that you might make to the other party about what you would like in return from them if you compromise on those aspects.

11. Be clear in your own mind as to what the consequences will be and what you will do if your minimum is not met by the other person.

12. If the person is willing to change their behavior toward you in a constructive way, is there something that you can reasonably offer to do for them in return?

13. In light of your relationship with the other party and your knowledge of them, give some thought in advance to what style of approach is most likely to encourage positive responses to your position. Will it help for you to be encouraging and constructive and try to engage in a joint search for solutions? Or will it be more productive if you take a firm stance from the outset, indicating absolutely clearly what you want and what will be the consequences if your wishes are not met or at least are

not met in full? The best style of approach may vary for different situations.

14. When, where, and how do you want to approach an issue to give yourself the best chance of getting a constructive response from the other party? For example, in most cases you will want to raise the subject at a time when everyone can give full attention to the discussion without distractions.

15. While you are looking for a good time to raise the topic, don't put off the moment forever! The perfect time will probably never happen. If you find yourself delaying too much, then select a specific time or occasion to raise the matter and keep to your commitment.

BUILDING RESPECT IS ESSENTIAL

Right now, think of a person in your working life with whom you feel a real sense of rapport. It can be a colleague or a supervisor or someone with whom you have management responsibility. There are many reasons why you may feel this way. There are lots of things you may like about that person, but in a business setting it's very difficult to like people unless you also respect them. For this reason, respect is a fundamental element of rapport.

As with other aspects of assertiveness, respect depends on knowing who you are and where you stand in an organization. There are no one-size-fits-all answers. For example, there are books that will tell you that you should never answer your own phone calls at work and that doing so will make you look unimportant. Instead, you should have an assistant screen your calls. In fact, you should have an assistant do a lot of things, such as scheduling, sorting mail, answering emails, and writing routine memos. Other books say that people gain respect by picking up their own calls or answering their own email. Building self-respect, as well as gaining respect, have everything to do with respecting others, knowing what works best for you, believing in yourself, and feeling comfortable with your individual style.

THE FOUR STEPS TO GAINING RESPECT IN BUSINESS

To show that you're a respectable person, be assertive in implementing the following steps. They're especially important when you are in the early or middle stages of your career.

First, maintain a busy schedule. Most successful and influential people are busy, well read, involved in several projects, have many contacts, and are always networking. As a person of credibility and respect, you should rarely be idle. When you find something that you are passionate about doing, getting involved and keeping busy will come naturally.

Second, show that you're a person of respect by placing yourself in important settings. Make an effort to attend a select a number of high-profile events and functions. People who know how to build rapport naturally like to be around other people. They like to see and be seen. They like to network; they enjoy being in the loop. One thing is for sure: You won't build rapport if there's no one around to do it with. So, assert yourself in the direction of socializing within your professional community.

Third, make an effort to spend time in the company of successful and well-regarded people. Take a sincere interest in them, both on a personal and professional level, and learn as much as you can from them. This can help you reach the next level as well as make a lasting impression on others. Who you know says a lot about who you are. When you learn to build rapport with successful individuals, you'll be amazed by the number of people who will want to build rapport with you.

Next, think carefully about your workspace and how it looks.

It's important to have a neat office, not just for the sake of appearance but because it will actually help you get more done. With respect to office furnishings and accessories, make "less is more" your guiding principle. In fact, with the introduction of new communications technologies, it could be argued that the importance of having an office at all has radically diminished. Tom Peters, one of the most influential business writers of the past fifty years, advises managers to spend as little time as possible in their offices. As Peters makes clear, the way to build rapport is by walking around and talking with people. Ask yourself what's the most assertive stance you can take with respect to your office.

As you can see, there's a lot to know about how to build rapport. Some people have this talent naturally, while others learn it by trial and error. For some, mastering this process can take years. As an assertive person, of course, you don't have much time to wait. In the next chapter we'll look at some exercises that can improve your rapport-building skills in the shortest possible time.

ACTION STEPS

1. The ideal description of your business relationships would be "mutual liking and trust." Make a list of all the significant relationships in your business life. Which fall under that category? More significantly, which do not? What action steps can you take to shift those relationships to reflect better communication and understanding?

2. How well do you speak of your own accomplishments? Do you tend to shy away from speaking openly about yourself? Do you tend to exaggerate your accomplishments? Test yourself by asking a friend to listen as you discuss those things about yourself that you are most proud of. Then ask your friend for honest feedback. Ask them were you too embarrassed? Too verbose? Ask them how you

might improve this skill. Then continue to practice listing your accomplishments in a way that is self-assured and confident.

3. Many people are uncomfortable with silence. Are you? If so, the next time you are in a conversation, make note of the silent moments. Try to stretch them and find comfort in them. Repeat this exercise frequently until you find yourself more comfortable with silence. Write about any insights that you gain by practicing this exercise.

4. The four steps to gaining respect in the business world are:

    1. Have a busy schedule.

    2. Place yourself in important settings.

    3. Spend time in the company of successful, well-regarded people.

    4. Keep a neat workspace.

Do you follow the four steps above? Which do you need to work on? When and how can you begin to improve that area of your life? Write out an action plan.

5. Respect is key. Make a list of all the attributes that you most respect in yourself. Then make a list of those that you need to work on and develop an action plan. Now think of someone whom you struggle to respect. Take some time to write out a list of attributes that they have that you do respect. Then focus on those attributes, and make note of any changes you have when engaging with them after doing so.

ACTION PLAN NOTES

Give the other person a fine reputation to live up to.
— Dale Carnegie

CHAPTER 4

Tactics for Assertive Rapport Building

I n this chapter we'll continue to explore how to build rapport with an emphasis on exercises you can practice on your own, as well as tactics you can try out with the people you meet every day in your work environment.

Let's be up front about one very important fact. Most nonassertive people are naturally rather shy. Some are moderately shy, and some are extremely shy. But if assertiveness is an issue in your life, the chances are you're not a naturally gregarious, life-of-the-party-style person. And there's nothing wrong with that. It just means that you have to be conscious of your personal style. You have to balance your natural tendency with something else—something that may not be as natural but that can be very beneficial to your life and career.

Even if you're a very self-contained and solitary person, there are people in the world with whom you'll find it easy to build rapport. In fact, there are probably a lot of people like that, regardless of what you're like as an individual human being. The difficulty comes when you need to build rapport with people who are very unlike you. Often these are people whose interests and backgrounds are different from yours. Individuals who think and talk and listen differently than you do.

You can count on the fact that you'll meet a lot of these diverse personalities in your working life. The higher up you move in an organization, the more diverse personalities you will encounter. In order to build a career that's both successful and enjoyable, you can and must learn how to build rapport with personalities that might otherwise have made you somewhat uncomfortable, not to mention those that would have driven you completely up the wall. In the next few pages we'll be looking at a number of the personality types you're likely to encounter. We'll then develop some tools and tactics to make sure that those encounters turn out in the best possible way.

FOUR DIFFICULT PERSONALITY TYPES

Since ancient times, human beings have classified one another according to certain basic temperaments or personality types. The Four Temperaments, also known as the Four Humors, may be the oldest of all personality profiling systems—yet these principles are still very useful and accurate today. They can be traced back to doctrines of the Egyptian and Babylonian cultures, in which physical and emotional health were connected with the elements—fire, water, earth, and air. These ideas were further refined by the Ancient Greeks, so that these ideas came to dominate Western thinking about human behavior and medical treatment for more than two thousand years. Imbalance among the "humors" expressed itself through various behaviors and illnesses. Treatments were based on restoring balance.

In keeping with these ancient principles, we're now going to look at four different categories of people; four difficult personality types that can create challenges in building rapport. While these aren't reflective of all personality challenges you might face on the job, each of them presents specific issues with regard to rapport building. You'll certainly find some of them easier to deal with than others, depending on what your own personality is like.

In fact, here are a couple of questions you should be asking yourself throughout this overview:

- Which one of these categories most resembles me?

- What challenges do I bring to people who are trying to build rapport with me?

- Most important, while I'm trying to find easy ways to get along with other people, what can I do to make it easier to get along with me?

The Ultradriver

The first personality type we'll discuss are the kind of people who are often described as hard drivers, peak performers, top achievers, or words to that effect. We'll call them "ultradriver." They see their business relationships as a hierarchy in which they're determined to reach the top. Even if they haven't reached that goal yet, they'll still do their best to be one rung above you on the corporate ladder.

Regardless of gender, there are some people who see life as a zero-sum game: For me to gain, you have to lose. Every meeting, every phone call, every email, and every courier package is another opportunity for dominance and intimidation.

It's not easy to build rapport with the ultradriver personality under any circumstances, and it's especially difficult when you're at the same level or below in the corporate hierarchy. But this kind of person is so common among high-level managers that you simply must learn how to get along with them. What needs to be done?

First, realize that the ultradriver's behavior patterns are based on ego needs. Some of these people secretly believe that they're actually inferior to everyone around them, while others truly are convinced of their own superiority. It doesn't really matter. Your main task is to find ways to service their ego needs. When you do this correctly, they'll be so gratified by what you've done that they'll become surprisingly compliant. In short, they'll like you. They'll appreciate the fact that you see the world as it really should be—with them on top. Once you've created rapport in this way, you'll be amazed at what a friendly person the ultradriver can turn out to be.

This sounds simple enough, but the hard part of dealing with the big ego of an ultradriver is keeping your own ego needs out of the encounter. To see how this works, consider the following example.

Randall is the owner of a company that supplies building supplies to customers around the world. It's not a glamorous business, but over the years it's been very successful. Randall is the kind of boss who keeps a very low profile. Rather than spend time at the country club or taking two-hour lunches, he likes to immerse himself in the nuts and bolts of the business (which is, quite literally, nuts and bolts). One of Randall's vice presidents is a man named Ben, a very different kind of person from Randall. Ben likes the power and prestige that comes with holding a high rank at a successful company. He enjoys going to the restaurants, golf tournaments, and industry functions that Randall shuns. Randall himself is quite comfortable with that. He knows that he likes to stay out of the limelight, but he also sees the value of someone like Ben, who brings the company's presence out into the world.

One day something very surprising happened. A close personal friend of Randall's took him aside and revealed that Ben was portraying himself as the CEO of the company. He didn't actually use those words, but in social settings Ben managed to convey the idea that he was the big boss. When Randall heard this, he thanked his friend for the information and said that he would speak to Ben about it.

Although Randall was surprised that Ben would misrepresent

his role in the company, the more he thought about it, the less surprised he actually felt. Ben, after all, was a person who needed to feel like he was the top dog. He couldn't really function unless he felt that way. And since he did do some valuable work, some space should probably be made for Ben's ego needs. Since those needs weren't going to go away, the only other alternative would be to fire him.

That same afternoon Randall asked Ben to come to his office. After a bit of small talk, Randall disclosed the rumor his friend had told him. "I've just heard something really strange," Randall said. "I understand you've been telling people that you're the head of the company—that you actually have my job."

As soon as the words were out of Randall's mouth, Ben began to stiffen up. He was caught, and he knew it. He was on the defensive, which was not a position in which he liked to find himself. Randall had to admit that he felt a certain amount of satisfaction in putting some brakes on this ultradriver. At the same time, though, Randall had decided not to make an ego investment in this confrontation. He wanted Ben to stop lying about his title, but he also wanted to keep Ben in the company for the company's own good.

As Ben sat there squirming, Randall said something that Ben didn't expect. "I'm not really all that surprised by what you've been doing," Randall said, "because, after all, there's really a lot of truth in it. We both know that you contributed mightily to the work here. In fact, your efforts have provided much of our success."

As Ben tried to decide what to say, Randall continued. "The problem is, Ben, it creates a lot of confusion when you talk like this, even if there is truth in it. It also causes a certain amount of pain to me. So I'd like to ask you to knock it off, for my sake and for the sake of the company. We both know how valuable you are around here, and that's what really matters. Do you understand what I'm trying to say?"

Actually, Ben still wasn't sure that he did understand what Randall was saying, but it didn't really matter. On the one hand, he was extremely grateful that he wasn't getting fired. On the other hand, his ego was ready to believe that what Randall said was actually true. In any case, Ben decided then and there to keep quiet about who did what in the company. To say he felt rapport with Randall would be putting it much too mildly. He felt tremendously grateful to Randall, and he also felt just a little bit fearful of him in a way that he had never experienced before.

As a general rule, what the ultradriver wants more than anything else is recognition for his or her talents and contributions. Once again, this desire may be based on insecurity, or it may come from genuine egotism. You don't have to figure that out. You're a businessperson, not a psychoanalyst. Don't get in a power struggle with an ultradriver. If they are making a real contribution to your enterprise, tell them so. Without question, that's the best way to build rapport with this type of ego-driven person.

Having said that, we also have to face the fact that sometimes ultradrivers leave you no choice other than to banish them, and you have to be able to do that, or they will eat you alive. From a historical point of view, one of the great ultradrivers of the twentieth century was General George S. Patton. Early in World War II, Patton did a great job leading troops in North Africa and Sicily. He did such a great job, in fact, that he started to act more like a king than a general. By that time, plans were under way for the Normandy invasion in June 1944. General Dwight Eisenhower realized that Patton couldn't be trusted to cooperate in a huge operation of that kind, so Eisenhower simply excluded Patton from taking part in the invasion. In an act that required a great deal of leadership and courage, he blatantly sidelined Patton, who felt angry and humiliated as a result. But Eisenhower understood both the strengths and weaknesses of the ultradriver personality. Once the invasion had taken place, he immediately began rebuilding rapport with Patton and quickly offered him command of a large body of troops on the Continent. Patton was still angry, but he couldn't resist the bone that was being thrown to him. That's the way it always is with an ultradriver. You've got to make them feel important, or else you've got to really put them in the doghouse for a while.

The Secret Agent

The opposite personality type of the ultradriver is not what you might expect. It's not someone with low self-esteem who hides in a cubicle somewhere. No, the opposite of the ultradriver is a personality that we can call the secret agent. The secret agent has many of the same ego needs as the ultradriver but is much less obvious about it. This is a type of person who wants to be moved up but wants to do it in a very secretive way. Secret agents are very politically astute within the corporate setting. They're very territorial. To win their confidence, you've got to make it very clear that you're not going to diminish them in any way. This is different from the ultradriver, who wants outright praise and recognition. You don't have to give the secret agent anything positive, but you do have to reassure them that you don't have anything negative in mind. For secret agents, negative means anything that might encroach on their territory.

When we spoke about Ben, the ultradriver, we saw how difficulties arose from Ben's habit of talking too much or, if not talking too much, certainly saying the wrong things. A secret agent will rarely behave in that manner. The problem with secret agents is they don't talk enough. They don't tell you things you need to know. Their natural tendency is to withhold information so that their possession of it can maximize their own sense of self-importance.

As a result, the goal of rapport building with secret agents is to draw them out; to create enough trust so that they emerge from their customary secretiveness. The best approach to take with a secret agent is to ask as many questions as possible. At the same time, you must make it clear that you have no hidden agenda for the information you hope to receive. You have no intention of using it to expand your own influence within the corporation, and you certainly have no desire to diminish the secret agent in any way.

Secret agents rarely achieve the highest levels of leadership positions. Those positions usually go to the ultradrivers. The truth is, though, secret agents don't really want to be the official leaders. They want to have their private fiefdoms in which they can exert absolute power without being in the glare of the spotlight. So don't feel you have to keep your own ambitions under wraps when you're talking with a secret agent. On the contrary: Let the secret agent know that you're aiming for the top, and let the secret agent also know that you'll depend on him or her to be an important power behind the throne.

The Eager Beaver

So far we've written about building rapport with what might be called "difficult" personalities. With the ultradriver and the secret agent, it's clear from the beginning that you have to make adjustments in your own personal style. To build rapport with these people, you have to understand their needs and learn how to meet them. There's another kind of person, however—eager beavers. These personality types seem to be so likable, so compliant, so eager to please, and you need an entirely different set of people skills to deal with them.

Usually eager beavers are new to the corporation. They can't wait to absorb the company culture, to go out to lunch with everybody, to work hard and get ahead. If you've been with the company for a while, you'll find the eager beaver looking up to you with undisguised admiration. The question is, how are you going to respond to that? You might not take it very seriously, you might be flattered, or you might try to take advantage of the eager beaver in some way. From the viewpoint of rapport building, however, the best thing to do is to recognize the strengths of the eager beaver and also the weaknesses. These are people who do indeed have many strengths. They have a lot of energy, they're usually very intelligent, and they buy totally into the collective enterprise of a corporation.

Here's the one thing to take note of when dealing with an eager beaver: Nobody, or almost nobody, remains an eager beaver forever. You need to know this, not just for your business's sake but for your own best interests as well. The key is, if you handle them poorly, high-energy eager beavers can quickly fall apart. They can go from being extremely helpful and efficient to being almost nonfunctional. They can change from being excited and naively confident to being hurt, depressed, and almost paralyzed. This all depends on how well you understand them and how well you put that understanding to use.

In the past few years, there have been several instances of journalists at major newspapers who got into trouble for fabricating or plagiarizing stories. One of the most flagrant of these stories involved a young reporter at the *New York Times* who seems to have been a classic eager beaver. Within the highly competitive culture of the newsroom, he presented himself as someone who was willing and able to work twice as hard as anyone else. He was the first one there every morning and the last to leave at night. In fact, there were many nights when he never did leave. He was literally living at his workstation, typing out copy at his computer terminal.

How did his supervisors respond to this eager beaver? Basically, they took his behavior at face value. He portrayed himself as somebody who was willing to do any job, no matter how much work was involved and no matter how impossible the deadline seemed to be. The senior editors simply shrugged their shoulders and gave him more work and more impossible deadlines. They figured, if that's what he wants, that's what we'll give him. He seems to be a young superman.

In hindsight, of course, those editors can probably see exactly what was happening. If the young eager beaver was beating impossible deadlines again and again, one of two things had to be happening. Either the deadlines weren't really impossible, or something not quite kosher had to be happening. Of course, it was the second of those options that proved to be true. The eager beaver was filing stories for the *New York Times* from all over the country, but he was never actually leaving New York City. In fact, sometimes he had never even left the *New York Times* building. His eagerness to please had turned into behavior that subverted the integrity of the whole company. What's more, he now felt that he himself was being exploited, even though he was the one who had begged to be given more work. All that enthusiasm had turned to anger. In his own mind, his unethical behavior was justified because he had been given an unrealistic workload.

There's a lesson here for rapport building with eager beaver personalities. Since they're not able to put on the brakes by themselves, you have to help them do it. Above all, don't just assume that they know what they're doing. That's definitely not the case. Don't let them burn themselves out, because if that happens they can really do a lot of damage to themselves, and perhaps to you as well. Rapport building with eager beavers is a matter of helping them pace themselves. They may feel bad at first. They may feel that you're trying to hold them back or that you want to keep them out of the limelight. They may even feel that you're jealous of their talent and energy. Unfortunately, if you let them run, burnout is inevitable, and that's bad for everyone.

The Burnout

The burned-out individual is another kind of person that's very frequently encountered in a corporate environment. What's more, you'll need a special set of people skills in order to build rapport with them. It may take some work, but it's usually worth doing. Very often these seemingly depressed individuals have some valuable knowledge and abilities. At the very least, they can give you insights on the corporate culture, which is especially important if you've just come on board. At best, they may be able to regain some energy and become real contributors. It all depends on whether you're able to rehabilitate someone who has more or less given up on him- or herself.

When you're dealing with someone who has lost enthusiasm and is just treading water, keep criticism to a minimum. In fact, this is a case when you should exclude criticism altogether from your rapport-building repertoire. Why shouldn't you criticize somebody who's obviously making a halfhearted effort? Because criticism is what they're used to, what they've come to expect, and even what they want.

They'll agree with you if you criticize them! They might not come out and say it, but on the inside you're just saving them the trouble of beating up on themselves. That's their comfort zone, and they've got to get out of that zone before they can be of any help to anybody. So be supportive. Express gratitude. Pat them on the back. Find a reason to say something good, and then keep saying it.

The greatest gift you can give someone who's burned out in the corporate environment is the gift of hope. Don't wait until they've done something good. Don't make that gift contingent on some goal or performance. Give it right now. This is something that many people don't understand about working with people. It's not a matter of saying "Here's what I want you to do, and here's what you'll get if you do it." Instead, it's rewarding even the slightest positive action right now. By doing so, you move the person toward the behavior you want. You create motivation and momentum. You get them moving under their own sense of power.

If you're part of a corporate environment, I guarantee you that at this moment there are at least three or four people who fall into the category of employee burnout. If you think about it for a moment, I'm sure you could name them right now. Fundamentally, it doesn't matter what level they're at. No matter what their level, the basic personality type is the same. They've given up hope. They're just going through the motions. They're washed up on the beach and the tide's not going to come in.

Think of a couple of these people who are in your workplace right now. You know who they are. Once you've done that, try this experiment. It's an experiment in rapport building and in people skills, but it's more than that. It's an experiment in you, in your being a good person.

Find something to say to those two or three people that's encouraging, reinforcing, and basically hopeful. Take a look at what they're doing right now and find something good to say about it. Do this not once but several times. You don't have to give this reinforcement every hour, every day, or even every week, but give it at least three times over a period of a month or so. Pay close attention to the results. You'll discover how much difference the encouragement makes, just as Dale Carnegie did. Most important, you'll begin to realize what positive impact good people skills can have on anyone and everyone. That's more than just building rapport. That's building success in the truest sense of the word.

QUESTIONS TO KEEP IN MIND

Building rapport with other human beings, whether they're difficult people or not, is not so different from any other endeavor. A certain amount of planning and foresight goes a long way. Ask yourself these questions as you consider how to build rapport with the people in your life.

What do you want to accomplish? It's essential to have clear results in mind. This is essential in every area, whether it's building your career or developing good relationships with the people in your life. What is the scenario you want to bring about? What is the outcome you want to achieve? It's important to think clearly about this, and it's even more important to take positive action based on your thoughts. All too often, people focus on what they desire to avoid instead of what they want to achieve. A very key people skill is the ability to move toward an identified destination rather than simply escaping an unwanted situation. The destination must be where you want to arrive. This is your purpose and your goal. What you want is much more important than what you don't want. Along these lines, be sure to state your desired result in positive terms. Don't say "I want to avoid a nine-to-five job." Instead, make the phrasing positive and proactive: "I want to be my own boss and set my own hours."

How will you evaluate your progress? Change is the one constant in the world. From minute to minute, nothing is the same physically, emotionally, and even spiritually. Whatever you may have intended, you need to look continually at the outcome of your actions to see whether you're on the right or the wrong track. If something isn't working, it's just common sense to try something different until you get the result you want. What evidence can you produce to show that you are moving toward your goals in your dealings with other people? In the absence of tangible evidence, there is no way to measure progress toward the achievement of the outcome. Do you have more acquaintances that you can honestly describe as friends? Does your phone ring more often than it used to? Are you spending less time alone and more time with others? These are specific, verifiable changes. They're real evidence of progress, not just feelings.

How can you adjust your actions in line with your evaluations? When you change your behavior, you should do so carefully. Take complete responsibility for your actions and the results. You can't depend on anyone else to make changes. All you can do is change your own thoughts and behaviors. Then you must observe and respond to the results, which can manifest themselves in the way the behaviors of others also change.

What can you do right now to get started? Once you know your desired outcome you will be motivated to move toward it. If you know your present behavior is not getting the results you want in your interpersonal relationships, you need to do something else. Moreover, you must be prepared to keep changing and adjusting your actions until there is evidence you are moving closer to your goals. With respect to taking any action, the key phase is *Do it now!*

Results are what matter. Every interaction between you and another person has two components. The first element is what you intend to communicate. The second element—which is much more important—is what the other person actually takes in. Sometimes these two elements are one and the same, but, unfortunately, that is often not the case.

People often assume that once they "say their piece," the job is finished. They assume that their message has been received. They hope that it has been understood and accepted—and if it hasn't, they tend to place the responsibility on the other party. However, in terms of effective people skills, your work as a communicator is only just beginning when you have finished speaking. You must determine the extent to which your words have not just been heard but have been understood. To do this, you must pay close attention to the response you're getting. If it is not the response you want, you need to vary your own communication until your interpersonal objective is achieved.

There are several major sources of misunderstanding in communication. The truth is, every human being has a different life experience associated with each word that's heard or spoken. What one person means by a word is very often quite different from what another person understands by it. A second source of misunderstanding arises from the nonverbal components of communication, including tone of voice and facial expression. People respond to these as much as if not more than what's actually said.

Your world is not my world. Or is it? Good communicators realize that the way they experience their lives may be very different from the experience of others. To put it another way, no two people live in exactly the same world. Every individual creates a unique model of the world and therefore inhabits a somewhat different reality from everyone else. Despite how it may seem, we do not respond directly to the world but to our experience of the world as we construct it. No one can say whether this experience corresponds to external reality or not—and it really doesn't matter. What does matter is the "in here" that we interpret as "out there." Your task is to move the person you're talking with into the world you inhabit. This is really a multifaceted process. You must engage your partner physically, mentally, and emotionally.

Words are an imperfect representation of experience. Just as each of us has a different experience of the world, the words we use further complicate our communication. Language is a code to represent things we see, hear, or feel. People who speak other languages use different words to represent the same things that English speakers see, hear, or feel. Also, since each person has a unique set of experiences that they have seen, heard, and felt in their lives, their words have different meanings from each of them. Finally, some people are much more adept at verbal communication than others. Of course, vocabulary and educational level are factors in this—and they, in turn, are affected by many variables, such as the type of school one attended and learning talents or disabilities. Effective communicators work to maximize their ability to express themselves. They also realize that even if they do maximize their skills, miscommunications are still bound to occur, even when the meaning seems "obvious."

Flexibility is always the key. Based on all the points above, it should be clear that the person with the highest degree of flexibility will be the most effective communicator. For example, if you have an extremely limited vocabulary, you will be able to communicate your message in a very limited number of ways. But the more words you know, the greater your options become. If someone doesn't understand what you're trying to say, therefore, you're able to find other ways to say the same thing. Choice is always better than no choice, and more choices are always preferable than fewer. This is true with regard not only to the number of words at your disposal but also to your range of emotions and even to the variety of clothes you wear. If what you are doing is not working, you should have the resources to vary your behavior and do something else.

ACTION STEPS

1. List an individual in your life who is most like each of the four personality types.

   Ultradriver: _____

   Secret agent: _____

   Eager beaver: _____

   Burnout: _____

   Do you judge any of these individuals in any way? If so, then perhaps you struggle with some of their attributes yourself. Reflect on each, and do an honest inventory of yourself, noting when you may behave like one or more of these four personality types. How might you shift that behavior to better serve yourself and those around you?

2. Make a list of those in your workplace with whom you find it easiest to build rapport. Take some time to examine why

you find them easy to communicate with. Then make a list of those with whom you struggle. What steps might you take to feel more comfortable with them? How might you begin to build rapport with them?

3. Have you ever suffered from burnout? What three steps can you take to prevent yourself from burning out again?

ACTION PLAN NOTES

*Expressing genuine interest in others—there's no better way
to make people interested in you.*

—Dale Carnegie

CHAPTER 5

Assertive Curiosity

A second essential people skill is assertive curiosity. People
are naturally curious. We're born with it! Isaac Singer,
Nobel Prize–winning author, once described life as a
novel that has good parts and bad parts. Like a novel, no matter
what you might say about it, everybody wants to see what's on
the following page. Everybody wants to learn what's going to
happen next. Everybody is inherently curious about the world,
and we should do everything we can to nurture that inborn
human characteristic and keep it alive.

This has special relevance in a corporate setting. Curiosity can
be of tremendous benefit to any manager who knows how to ignite the inborn curiosity of his or her team. In the next few pages,
we'll explore strategies and tactics for making the best possible
use of other people's curiosity. Most important, we'll see why the
key to doing that lies in keeping your own curiosity alive and well.

THE STORY OF MICHELLE

Let's look at an example of how this works. Michelle is an investor
relations executive with a large multinational corporation. Her

job is a very interesting one, and it depends heavily on her having a healthy sense of curiosity. Basically, she keeps in touch with people who are large investors in her company and she tries to learn if they have any particular needs or concerns.

Many, though not all, of the large investors are elderly people for whom loneliness is a real concern. At this point in their lives, they have a lot of money and not much else going on. When Michelle contacts them, they want to talk about their investment, but they also want to feel that she's taking a real interest in their lives. The conversations that result from this may not seem like conventional business discussions, but Michelle quickly learned that talking about someone's grandchildren for half an hour can make a very positive difference in building trust and loyalty. So she's learned to be genuinely curious about the people she talks with and about what they have to say. Often this has meant delving into topics that might not have seemed all that interesting or relevant at first glance. But it's amazing how taking the time to get to know someone can build customer relations and help you achieve success.

When Michelle was tasked with training a new employee to help her with her work, she had a chance to reflect on what curiosity really means as a people skill in a business environment. Like Michelle, you may be a manager who wants to motivate your team to learn as much as possible as quickly as possible. Or you yourself may be a new hire who's curious about your company. You want to put your curiosity into action in ways that will benefit you and your employer. Whether you're a seasoned manager or a new employee, what you're really looking for is assertive curiosity. That's a very unique and somewhat complex frame of mind. It includes no less than ten separate but closely related elements. By putting them into action, you can instantly maximize the role of curiosity in your people skills repertoire. Let's look at these points one by one.

POINT 1: MAKING ASSERTIVE CURIOSITY AN EMOTIONAL EXPERIENCE

First, you need to realize that assertive curiosity is an emotional as well as an intellectual experience. When you're dealing with another person, this is the difference between really creating a sense of shared discovery and just politely inquiring about one thing or another. If there's one word that describes this special kind of energy, the word is *passion*. Assertive curiosity is more about passion than about simply gathering facts. It's not only motivating yourself to learn but also teaching yourself to do it in ways that are meaningful, memorable, and effective. It's about caring for what you want to learn, feeling real excitement for it, and conveying that excitement to the people around you.

How did Thomas Edison manage to get over one thousand patents from the U.S. Patent Office? The engine that powered all those discoveries was infinite, unlimited curiosity. Edison wasn't a theorist. He was what's called an empirical thinker. He liked to see how things worked in the real world. It didn't really matter whether the real world worked the way he thought it would. Even if one of his experiments came out differently than he expected, he never regarded this as a failure. He never spoke of "failed experiments" in the conventional scientific jargon. Every experiment was a success, because he always found out something new. If it was something other than what he anticipated, so much the better. What's more, Edison was able to transfer this curiosity to all the people who worked with him. That's what made him an assertively curious person.

POINT 2: SEEING YOURSELF AS A STUDENT AND PURVEYOR

Of course, assertive curiosity is about substance as well as emotion. So the second point involves seeing yourself both as a student and as a purveyor of real knowledge. It's about doing your best to keep on top of your field, by gathering information both inside and outside your areas of expertise, and being at the leading edge as often as possible. This doesn't mean spending hours every day on the internet, in the library, or poring over professional journals. Assertive curiosity is something much more dynamic than that. It's about bridging the gap between theory and practice. It's about leaving the ivory tower and immersing yourself in a particular field. It's talking to the experts and authorities inviting people to talk with you as you become an authority.

Nobel Prize—winning physicist Richard Feynman was like a modern-day Edison in some respects. Feynman's work, however, was in the hidden world of quantum mechanics and cosmology. There was also a very practical side to Feynman. He once said that there is a sure way to tell whether someone is a real expert or just posing as one. It all depends on how often they say three very important words, "I don't know." If a person has the answer to every question, if there's seemingly nothing on a particular topic that they don't thoroughly understand, then you know you've got a phony on your hands. When somebody obviously knows a lot but is still able to admit that they don't know everything, that's the mark of true confidence and authority. Of course, Feynman added an extremely vital corollary to that principle that definitely applies to assertively curious individuals. While they're more than willing to admit they don't know, they also have a very strong intention to find out. Assertively curious people are eager to be challenged, and they'll challenge others in return. They want to get the facts, and they know they haven't got all of them yet. What's more, they know they'll never get all the facts, and they're very happy about that.

POINT 3: INTERACTIVE LISTENING

Drawing upon this, our third point concerns the operational, interactive component of assertive curiosity. It's listening, questioning, being responsive, and remembering that every human being is different from every other. It's about eliciting responses and drawing out people who are naturally quiet. It's about finding what's best in people while also respecting their limits and being professional at all times.

When people are speaking to you, do you listen with full attention or are you distracted by their appearance, their phrasing, or other details? Is listening a matter of waiting for the other person to stop so that you can start talking, or is it a skill that you genuinely want to develop? It's amazing how rare good listeners really are—and by becoming one of those rare people, you can take a big step toward making yourself a truly skilled communicator.

How do you react when someone says something that you disagree with? Are there certain topics or certain people that you immediately find irritating? The truth is, we all have our hot buttons—but here again, an important aspect of people skills is to be in control and to accept responsibility. When someone says something that seems totally off the wall, he or she may indeed be an uninformed person. But it's not your responsibility to inform the world of that fact. Your responsibility is to respond with coolness, calm, and control—in a word, with skill.

The title of Dale Carnegie's most famous book is *How to Win Friends and Influence People*. It's a title that's known around the world and its simplicity is one of its strengths—but to really understand that title, we need to look very closely at one word. Surprisingly, that word is *and*. In ordinary conversation, *and* is just a linking word—a conjunction. But here those three letters have a more important function. *And* in the title of Dale Carnegie's book really means "in order to." The two parts of the title don't just coexist—one part grows from the other. It's not just a matter of making friends and influencing people. Making friends gives you the power to influence people. In the fewest possible words, gaining affection confers respect. It's not rocket science! It's simple. Not necessarily easy, but definitely uncomplicated.

Part of your commitment as a truly interactive listener

involves letting go of some of the negative set pieces that so many of us mistake for real conversation. Very simply put, don't criticize, condemn, or complain. Period. Why not? Well, do you enjoy listening to other people's complaints? Does hearing someone condemn someone else endear you to that person? Does hearing a list of criticisms from someone incline you to be positively influenced by them? I think the answers to these questions are very self-explanatory.

Instead of criticizing or complaining, create in yourself feelings of appreciation, gratitude, and genuine interest in other people. Don't do this because you want to be a Pollyanna. Do it out of positive self-interest. Once again, how do you feel around people who are positive and appreciative? Chances are, those are the kinds of people you'll want for your friends. And as Dale Carnegie showed, friends are the people who influence us. We generally want to forget about people who are habitually negative, but genuinely positive people are not just memorable—they're literally unforgettable.

What's the best way to show appreciation, gratitude, optimism, and other positive feelings? Once again, what you say and how you listen can be canceled out by how you look—so smile! What could be simpler? There's really no need to go very deeply into the benefits of smiling, but as discussed earlier, research shows that smiling—that is, flexing the muscles of the face—stimulates the production of certain neurochemicals in the brain that are associated with feelings of pleasure and well-being. At the most basic biological level, smiling is good for you.

And laughing may be even better than smiling. More than twenty years ago, Norman Cousins wrote a best-selling book describing how he watched movie comedies to deal with a serious illness. Since then, there have been many studies of the physical and emotional effects of laughter. One very interesting study tracked the frequency with which people laugh at various stages of life. At the age of three, we laugh a lot—hundreds of times a day, in fact. From then on, however, there's a gradual lessening of laughter over the course of many years. But then something very interesting happens. Some people start laughing more, and others stop laughing altogether.

Part of this may be a matter of genetics—but remember, an essential aspect of character is taking 100 percent responsibility. It may be that it's simply "natural " to become unhappier as we grow older. But that doesn't mean you have to let it happen. It may also be natural to become physically weaker and to gain weight, but millions of people have made it a priority to resist those processes. In the same way, you can make a commitment to keep your emotions positive just as you can to keeping your body healthy. But *commitment* is a key word. It doesn't happen by itself. It doesn't happen easily. You just have to make it look like it does!

Once again, there's nothing especially complicated about this. Usually it's just a matter of asking the right questions and really wanting to hear the answers. It can be as easy as saying "That sounds interesting. How can I help?" or "I've been thinking about something new. I'd like your opinion." Nothing is more inspiring to employees than having a manager ask for their feedback. How often, though, does that actually happen in the corporate world? Assertive curiosity doesn't mean just finding answers to problems. It's really about finding out what people think. When you do that, you'll be surprised at how many problems you can quickly eliminate. You'll be even more surprised by the number of problems that never come up in the first place.

POINT 4: BEING INTERACTIVE WITHOUT AN AGENDA

Assertive curiosity is about being interactive with people without having a fixed agenda. It's about being flexible in adjusting to other people's interests and having the confidence to admit that another point of view might be just as valid as your own.

Sometimes it means accomplishing only half of what you wanted from a meeting or a phone call but still feeling good about what you've learned. It means striking a creative balance between being an eager questioner and a patient teacher. It's about balancing your own curiosity with another person's need to learn.

In many areas Dale Carnegie was hugely ahead of his time, and one of the clearest examples of this is the way he stressed paying attention to other people's wants and needs and being aware of both verbal and nonverbal clues. That means being curious about what other people want and using those desires as a way to make a connection. The fact is, most people won't tell you what they really want unless you ask them, but how many of us ever bother to ask? The way around this is quite paradoxical. If you're really interested in what another person cares about, the best way to access that information is by sharing something about yourself. As you do so, though, you need to remember that you're only doing it as a way of inspiring the other party to talk. Don't get so caught up in your own story that there's no room for anyone else to say anything.

In order to share a personal story of your own as a way of building trust and eliciting information from another party, there are just a few points you need to keep in mind. First, always begin the conversation in a friendly and unthreatening manner. This is especially important if you're in a supervisory role, when people are naturally hesitant to open up to you. Generally it's best to be very explicit about this. Make it clear that the conversation will be off the record, or ask permission to share a piece of personal information. This is all part of really seeing the situation from the other person's point of view. Then make sure that the information you share is conveyed in a dramatic and interesting way, so that they'll feel inspired to do the same. For example, it's not very exciting to hear someone say, "Someday I'd like to have my own business." Compare that with "I've always dreamed of owning an elegant little boutique where I could sell really elegant clothes."

The second alternative is more than just a business plan. It's sharing a dream. And when you share one of your dreams, the person you're speaking with may find the courage to share one of theirs. This is what you really want to have happen when you're an assertively curious manager.

There are an infinite number of questions you can ask people in order to get them talking and sharing information about themselves. As we've seen, sometimes the best start is to reveal something about yourself, but the deeper purpose should be to ignite the other party's curiosity about things they may have simply taken for granted and accepted. Here are some sample questions that can serve that purpose. The chances are, a manager or supervisor in your workplace has never asked questions like this. Even if someone wanted to ask about these things, perhaps they seemed too personal or not businesslike. But they can be very important for creating an atmosphere of assertive curiosity. As you read these questions, you will begin to see how valuable they can be for helping people to find out about themselves and adopt an attitude of curiosity toward their lives. In fact, they'll probably help you to do much the same thing.

- What is the history of your family name?

- What part of the world is your family from?

- What is the linguistic derivation of your name?

- Where do you live? How do you like living there?

- What are some of the things that you enjoy doing with your family?

- What do you like and dislike about the kind of work you're doing in the company?

- How did you get your start with this organization?

- Tell me about some places you like to travel.

- Where is the last place you went for a vacation? What were your impressions?

- What sports do you enjoy?

- What are your hobbies?

- What do you like to do in your free time?

- What are your ideas on how our company could be changed for the better?

- If you could wave a magic wand and change one thing today, what would it be?

- What would you like to learn about in the next year? In the next week? Today?

- What are some obstacles you've had to overcome?

- What advice would you give a teenager who wanted to enter this line of work?

When you ask open-ended questions like these, you're exercising your curiosity. Couple this with active listening skills and you are demonstrating assertive curiosity and inspiring others. The choice is always yours.

POINT 5: SHARE YOUR PERSONAL STORIES WITH FLARE

The fifth point about assertive curiosity concerns the importance of personal style. We've seen how this works in terms of sharing your hopes and dreams. You've got to put some drama into them. You've got to make them exciting and heartfelt, as if you're sharing an important secret. The importance of this should be very obvious. How can you ignite curiosity in another person if you yourself don't seem very interesting? So often in meetings or presentations, speakers try to portray themselves as if they have all the answers. Even when they ask for questions from the audience, there's usually no sense of spontaneity or drama.

Let's be very clear about this—there's nothing less interesting than a know-it-all (even if the person actually does happen to know a great deal). On the other hand, when managers make it clear that they are also seeking to learn and that their sense of curiosity is still alive and well, they are much more inspiring leaders. An assertively curious person is like the leader of an orchestra. There have to be some theatrics involved. If you watch the conductor of a major orchestra, you'll see exactly what this means. It's not just about telling the instrumentalists which notes they ought to be playing at a particular moment. It's helping them to play in that moment as if they are discovering and expressing those notes for the very first time. When you know how to use curiosity in this way, you'll bring out the best in everyone, including yourself.

POINT 6: HUMOR

Humor is the sixth component of assertive curiosity, and it goes along with the sense of style that we've just been discussing. We've said that assertively curious people are very frank about how much they don't know. As a result, they often have a finely developed sense of self-deprecating humor. Humor and curiosity go together, because both depend on the pleasure of surprise and the unexpected. Humor isn't just a tactic of an assertively curious person; it's a natural characteristic. But in a practical sense, humor does create the kind of relaxed atmosphere that makes everyone want to listen and learn.

Before we leave the topic of humor, we should mention that it's one of the most elusive of all people skills. It's one of the most difficult skills to learn and master, and there's a very simple reason for that. Most people don't really think they have anything to learn about humor. Most people think they already know how to be funny, or at least how to appreciate a funny person or situation. Very few people will admit that they don't have a highly developed sense of humor. Yet how many people do you know who really have the ability to make you laugh? Conversely, do you have the ability to bring laughter to other people? Answering that question honestly can take some courage. But if it causes you to realize that your humorous quality isn't what you thought, there's still hope. Again, the solution lies in just being very honest. There was a gentleman who participated in some Dale Carnegie training, and when he heard this discussion of humor, he really took it to heart. He realized that despite what he might have thought, he actually didn't have a very good sense of humor. He wished he did, of course, but he wanted to face the truth. So at the next meeting of his class, he stood up and somewhat sadly announced the truth. He just said, "I'm not a funny person. I'm just not funny." And of course everybody laughed!

POINT 7: RECOGNIZING WHAT OTHERS NEED TO LEARN

Assertive curiosity means recognizing not only what other people want to learn but what they need to learn as well. Then it means sparking their curiosity to go ahead and learn it. Accomplishing this can take many forms. It can mean forwarding someone an article from the internet or leaving a book or a magazine on someone's desk. But it has to be done without an agenda on your part. This is especially true if you're in a supervisory role. Remember how difficult it was to read the books that were assigned to you in school? There's something about genuine learning that seems to be contradicted by being ordered to learn.

This is an area where a bit of reverse psychology can be very effective. When you give someone a book or article to read, you should be very explicit about the fact that you have no expectations or agenda that they'll actually do so. Really emphasize that point. You might say something like this: "If you ever have a moment, I think you might find this article useful. I know I did." And that's all you say. Leave it at that. You have to relinquish your own agenda completely if you want to create curiosity in the other individual. You have to be very assertive about that, and the assertiveness needs to be directed at yourself. Otherwise you're just engaging in a not-too-subtle form of manipulation, which has nothing in common with effective people skills.

POINT 8: REINFORCE WITH INSTITUTIONAL SUPPORT

Assertive curiosity has to be supported by the company culture as a whole. This means strong and visionary leadership, of course, but also tangible institutional support, including resources, personnel, and funds. Curiosity needs to be reinforced throughout the organization, from the CEO to the mailroom. It needs to be reflected in what is said and written, but more important, by what is done. You may be an assertively curious manager. You may really care about engendering authentic curiosity in your team, but if you're a lone voice in the midst of an essentially conformist environment, your impact is going to be limited.

So take a hard look at how your company responds to people

who ask unexpected questions and who come up with surprising answers. What systems are in place to support that kind of assertive curiosity and to reward it when it takes place? We tend to think of people skills in terms of what happens between two individuals or within a small group. But sometimes there are things that need to be done on the macro level that will make individual interactions much more effective.

POINT 9: MENTORING BY SENIOR MANAGEMENT

The ninth point is really a specific application of the previous point. Senior management should mentor curiosity for team members. Through a mentoring relationship, managers can see very clearly how well team members are seeking to expand their vision. With this insight, managers can make curiosity a factor in employee evaluation, recognition, and promotion. At the same time, lack of curiosity needs to be addressed through training and development books. This does not mean that there should be an official "department of curiosity" within the corporate structure. However, there should be a way of giving employees time and motivation to explore new ideas and points of view.

A classic example of how powerful this can be is the legendary Skunk Works division of the Lockheed Martin aircraft corporation. This was an unofficial department of the company, the sole purpose of which was to explore new ideas and eccentric or innovative approaches to problem solving. For more than fifty years, this division produced some of the most innovative concepts in the history of aviation. The success of this entire enterprise, however, was based on nothing more than the importance of curiosity and the power of junior and senior employees working together in an unstructured, no-pressure environment. For example, the whole technology of stealth design for military aircraft emerged from the Skunk Works. Engineers found the mathematical key to the stealth design buried within an obscure physics journal originally published in Russian. Oddly, the bureaucratic Russian military had never made use of the principle, despite urgings from the article's Russian author. Even more amazing is the way the first stealth plane was tested. The plane was housed in a secret, unlighted hangar full of bats. When the bats couldn't detect the plane's presence and crashed into it in the darkness, the engineers knew they had a successful design. It's very hard to imagine that a testing system using bats could have been thought of in a conventional research and development book. It required an institutional commitment to curiosity, in a setting that was outside the official company profile. In fact, for many years the existence of the Skunk Works was not even acknowledged by Lockheed Martin, nor did the U.S. government acknowledge the planes that came out of it.

POINT 10: CREATE A FUN ENVIRONMENT

Finally, the tenth principle of assertive curiosity, and perhaps the most important: Assertive curiosity should be fun. The rewards should be spontaneous and intrinsic. You should feel the excitement of wanting to explore a new topic, or see that you've kindled that excitement in one of your colleagues or coworkers. Assertively curious managers aren't doing it for the money. Curiosity is simply a part of who they are, and really curious people can't imagine doing anything else. Take the atmosphere at Google. Employees are encouraged and empowered to be curious, to explore, and to have fun. The results are an incredibly successful organization with happy and loyal employees.

A good way to glimpse the power of curiosity is to consider its opposite, which is boredom. Boredom is a feeling rarely experienced by small children. It's the sense that your creative, or even subversive, energies are being completely stifled. It's the way you feel when you have to sit up straight through a long class on something that holds no interest for you. That's not the right way to experience education, and it's certainly not the best way to live your life. We began this chapter with the idea that life is like a book and you don't want to reach the end. That may be true, but are you a person who's really interested in what you're reading, or are you just afraid of what might happen if you get to the last page? Answering that question is itself an example of assertive curiosity. It's the kind of question that deserves some thought on your part, and it's also something that you can inspire others to think about.

The ten points we've covered in this chapter can most certainly help you do that. But we've far from exhausted the subject of assertive curiosity. We'll continue our discussion in chapter 6.

ACTION STEPS

1. On a scale from 1 to 10, how much assertive curiosity do you have for the work that you do and for the individuals with whom you engage at work?

   1   2   3   4   5   6   7   8   9   10

   Very little   *Some*   *Quite a bit*   *A great deal*

2. Being assertively curious involves having flexibility and interest in the needs of others. Sometimes cultivating the desire to focus on the needs of others takes conscious commitment and practice. During the next week, choose at least one person a day whose needs you commit to focusing on. Write about any insights that you have gained by practicing this exercise.

3. It is important to be proactive by encouraging and enforcing learning among your staff. Write out a One-Year Learning Track for your team. Be sure to get their input and include their desires and interests. Then take the necessary action as required.

4. Creating fun and having a good sense of humor are two important traits to cultivate when developing your assertive curiosity. They are also choices that will uplift your spirit and enhance your daily exchanges. Are you having fun at work? Do you laugh a lot? Make a point of adding more fun and humor to your day. Keep a record of what you do and of any changes that you notice in response to making this commitment.

ACTION PLAN NOTES

Never underestimate the power of enthusiasm.
—Dale Carnegie

CHAPTER 6

Maximizing Assertive Curiosity in Business

B ased on what you learned in chapter 5, you should now see that assertive curiosity has many benefits, both as a trait of your own and as a quality you can develop in your team members. We've already discussed some of the people skills that can help you reach those objectives. Now, at the start of this chapter, we'll sharpen our focus a bit. We'll look at the things you absolutely must do as a manager to maximize assertive curiosity in a corporate setting. Please pay close attention to the four items we're going to cover now. These are the essentials—the "must-haves." These are the elements that really make the difference between a culture of complacency and a winning team.

THE FOUR ESSENTIAL ELEMENTS OF ASSERTIVE CURIOSITY

ELEMENT 1: *Frequent Contact*

Assertive curiosity depends on just a few vital components in the relationship between managers and employees. The most important of these is really very simple—it's frequency of contact.

Assertive curiosity requires face-to-face meetings with team members continually. In fact, you should be in touch every day if possible. This kind of concern lets you see who deserves praise at a given moment and who needs help. It shows your commitment, and it encourages your team members to think about what they can do in return.

In order to make this personal contact happen, you should schedule time every week for an individual meeting or for group interaction when team members can just get to know each other. A good time for this to happen is at the start of the workday. Perhaps once a week, for example, team members might be willing to come in twenty or thirty minutes early to catch up on what's been happening in their work and in their lives. This works best when everyone participates. Assertive curiosity is enhanced when it's a team effort rather a solo enterprise. Like all people skills, curiosity should be a collaborative and social experience, not a competitive and isolated one.

In order to make these informal meetings successful, it's best to have an agreed-upon topic that's neither too narrow nor too broad. If there's no topic for the meeting, there's a danger that people will just sit there waiting for someone to break the ice. That someone would likely be you, their manager or senior person in the group. If this happens, the meeting will result in an interaction that will become too formal; one in which everyone ends up following your lead. On the other hand, a topic that's too narrowly defined might prevent people from speaking about what's really on their minds. They might think their concerns are off topic, so they'll just keep quiet. The real purpose of having a topic for group interactions is not to solve that particular problem but to use the topic as a starting point for a discussion in which assertive curiosity gets put into action.

In a group setting like this, assertive curiosity becomes genuinely interactive. Team members develop and share questions, insights, and solutions. It's a good chance to learn how others think as well as how your own thought processes work. Within that framework, here are some specific guidelines for an effective group discussion. These are shared principles and responsibilities that should be defined and agreed to by each team member.

First and foremost, everyone should make a commitment to attend and be on time for the meetings. Team members should understand that the purpose here is not to stand out or win an argument. Friendly disagreements are acceptable and even desirable, but personal criticism should be avoided.

At the first meeting, decisions can be made about the group's goals, how often meetings will take place, how progress can be evaluated, and how any conflicts can be resolved. It's often a good idea to choose a new person to lead the discussion during each session. The group may feel more comfortable, however, if you, as the senior manager, were to take on that role every week. You know your group and can decide what would be the most beneficial.

Let's look at an example of how a meeting like this might proceed. We'll assume that the topic for the week is communication within the corporate setting. The leader of the discussion begins by asking if anyone can think of some obstacles that get in the way of people communicating effectively about work-related issues. If nobody responds, the discussion leader should share an experience of his or her own. This is a basic tool of assertive curiosity, and it usually primes the pump for others to come forward.

In any discussion of communication issues, a very common theme is the divergence of communication styles that can exist among individuals. For example, one person might be more comfortable with written communications, while another prefers speaking on the phone or personal meetings. Differences like these can become a problem when a manager prefers one style of communication, while a team member is more comfortable with another.

The end of the week is a good time for you as a manager to take a team member aside and check up on how things are going. It's a chance for you to ask questions one-on-one, and also to encourage employees to ask you about whatever is on their minds. Assertive curiosity begins with knowing what you don't know and then taking action to get that information.

You and your team members need frequent updates on individual responsibilities as well as on what's happening in the company as a whole. Without impinging on the privacy of team members, you should schedule appointments to observe team members actually doing their jobs. The intention here should be toward mentoring, support, and assertive curiosity. It shouldn't be like spying! This is a chance for you to assess and assist team members in whatever way they need help. At the same time, it's an opportunity for employees to make suggestions within the context of their everyday work environment.

ELEMENT 2: *Time Management*

We've seen how important it is to schedule group meetings, and also for you as a manager to spend time with individual team members. As you're thinking about scheduling interactions like these, it's a good idea to consider the issue of time management in general. As an assertively curious manager, one of the most important questions you can ask is "How much time do you need?" We can refer to this question as "time on task," and it should be brought up in every discussion of workplace issues. Learning to use time well is critical for both managers and team members. The fact is that people need help learning effective time management. Allocating realistic amounts of time means greater productivity. How a company and a manager define time expectations can establish the basis of peak performance for all.

Regarding time management, a good rule of thumb is "Expect more and you will get more." High expectations are important for everyone, especially in light of one of the corporate world's most firmly established laws: Work expands to fill the time available. Expecting team members to complete a task within a designated time frame can be a self-fulfilling prophecy, especially when you hold similar high expectations for yourself.

Without doubt, the single most effective time management tool is for team members to keep logs of how they spend their time each workday. In asking people to do this, you should be sure to put it in the context of assertive curiosity. Instead of presenting the time log as a form of intrusive scrutiny into what people are doing every second of the day, make it clear that this is just a way of exercising healthy curiosity about how things get done. The results are likely to be interesting and surprising.

Creating a Time Log

John, for example, is the owner of a film editing and postproduction facility in Los Angeles. He employs a team of editors who work on Hollywood movies as well as smaller, independently produced projects. Much of the work is done at night, and even for experienced night workers there's a tendency to become less than efficient at three or four in the morning. John wanted his team members to create time logs as a way of dramatizing the need for better work habits, but he knew there was danger in simply ordering them to do so.

Instead he came up with a novel way of introducing the topic. He bought some inexpensive stopwatches at a sporting goods store and passed them out to his team. Then he asked if everyone would agree to watch one of the professional football games that were going to be televised that weekend. As a special assignment, he asked his people to keep a time log of how much of the telecast was actual football action and how much was taken up by commercials or other breaks in the game. As their football time logs revealed, the action portion of the games comprised less than seven and a half minutes of the three-hour telecast.

Based on this information, it was easy for John to suggest try-ing something similar with time logs of the editing work. In fact, the editors looked at it almost as a game. They wanted to see how little actually got done over the course of an eight-hour shift. But once the logs were completed, everyone saw that a serious point was being made. The results were not quite as striking as the football time logs, but there was certainly not an optimal use of the available time. Through this assertively curious exercise, team members understood that changes had to be made. Because John had exercised creative people skills, the lesson was conveyed without negative feelings on anyone's part.

As a time log will reveal, different people work well in many different ways. Your awareness of this fact should be reflected in the way you discuss the time logs and in the larger expectations you have for one individual or another. Brilliant thinkers in the conference room may be much less effective in face-to-face deal-ings with clients or customers. Team members rich in hands-on experience may not do so well in presentations or in preparing written reports. People need the opportunity to find out where their talents lie and to use them in the ways that work best. Then, as time passes, they can be motivated to move into areas that don't come so naturally.

ELEMENT 3: *Seek Help from Management*

As a manager, you have primary responsibility for being assertively curious about your team and for improving and expanding their skills. But you need and deserve a lot of help. In particular, upper management has the power to shape an environment that is favorable to curiosity and achievement. You as a manager should make this clear to your supervisors.

When this exciting, assertively curious environment starts to come into being, managers and executives begin to think of them-selves as educators, not just as bosses. What specific qualities must the environment have? Adequate resources are put into creating opportunities for managers and team members to reflect and act on their mutual concerns. Managers receive support and are given time for the development of new ideas and approaches. The most crucial factor, however, is a strong sense of purpose. Setting goals is fundamental. This is necessary first for the organization as a whole, and then for each individual team member. This topic of goal setting is so central that we should spend a few moments thinking about it and seeing how goal setting is really an expression of assertive curiosity.

ELEMENT 4: *Goal Setting—Asking the Right Questions*

It is best to begin with some questions. What do you like to do? What are your interests? What are you truly passionate about? Ask yourself these questions, and ask your team members as well. Be sure to make it clear that the answers to these questions don't have to be work related, at least not initially.

Next, however, you'll want to ask how these passionate interests can find applications in the workplace. How can your interests benefit the company's profitability, which will advance your own career in the process? Be aware, however, that you're probably not the only person in the world, or even in your company, who has these talents. How can you be unique? How can you be better? As you scan the corporate environment, what do you see? Where do you fit? Where do you see opportunity? Those are big questions, and they're the kinds of questions that assertively curious people naturally ask in order to implement their goals.

Whenever you think about goals, there are other questions you should ask. These questions deal with the time issues we spoke about a moment ago. How long will it take to realize your goals? How will you measure your progress during that period?

Once you've identified your talents, translated them into specific goals, and put them into a time frame, there are still some more questions to ask. Be sure to consult with your colleagues and coworkers. What do they think of your goals? This is also a chance for you to ask them about their own aspirations.

Whenever you're thinking about goals, whether for yourself as an individual or for your team, understand that achieving your objectives will be difficult. If they're not difficult, you should ask whether these are indeed worthwhile goals. A real goal should be hard. It should test your will. Your resolve should be challenged. When that happens, will you double your efforts or run for shelter?

Ultimately, there is a very deep question you must ask: Are your goals driven by ego or by a higher sense? Is your goal superficial, or will it really benefit your work and your life? Improvement is the key idea here. When the goal is realized, you should be a lot better off than before. This doesn't only mean you'll earn a bigger salary. While more money is admittedly very important, there could also be intangibles that will enhance your situation after your goals have been achieved. What are those intangibles? How can you identify them and use them to increase your motivation? How can they get you from where you are now to where you really want and need to be?

Reaching Your Goals

Although spending time on goals and goal setting is not unusual in books on personal development or management training, goals are rarely linked to ideas like assertiveness or curiosity. In fact, the very importance of goal setting has led to its being discussed in very predictable ways. People ask, "What are your goals?" and it seems that whoever can list the most goals wins. But this isn't really the point. Making a list of goals can be fun, but there's not much point in listing all the things you want when you may never get there. What people really need to ask is "What will you do to make sure you reach your goals?" That's assertive curiosity.

Too many people treat goal setting like leaving on a dream vacation, without a map of how to reach the destination. It's one thing to dream about where you want to go, but you've got to know whether to go north or south. Maps, of course, are usually on paper, or today they may also be on a computer screen, a GPS, or your cell phone. You should use all of these mediums in order to take the all-important step of writing down your goals. They should be written not just as informal notes to yourself but as a carefully organized plan of action. Do this for yourself, and encourage your team members to do the same.

Aligning Your Goals with Your Values

As you begin to write out a goal, make sure it's something you really want. Be sure that is it not just something that sounds good or something you think you ought to want. When setting goals, remember that they must be consistent with your values. If you don't know what your values really are, now's a good time to ask yourself about them in an assertively curious way. Do the same for the members of your team. As you encourage them to write down their goals, encourage them also to think about what they believe in and how they came to have those beliefs. In this way, goal setting can become a powerful people skill.

For example, if someone on your team states that he or she wants to triple his or her income, feel free to compliment him or her on her ambition. You then need to ask how hard they want to work in order to achieve that goal. Is he or she willing to come in on weekends, for example, in order to put together a new presentation or to do some independent research? Perhaps spending that extra time at the office would contradict another goal, such as being with his or her family as much as possible.

It's a good idea to ask yourself about your goals in at least six different areas of your life: your business, your family, your finances, your physical health, your education, and your spiritual perspective. By gaining clarity in each of these areas, you will become a more complete person and you'll find that your skills in dealing with other people will be strengthened as well.

State Your Goals in the Positive

Always write your goals in the positive instead of the negative. Once again, do this yourself and encourage others to do the same. Think about what you want, not about what you want to leave behind. Part of the reason for writing down your goals is to create a set of instructions for our subconscious mind to carry out. The subconscious is a very efficient but somewhat limited tool. It cannot make the distinction between thought and physical reality, and it does not make judgments between right and wrong. Its only function is to carry out its instructions. The more positive instructions you give it, the more positive results you will get. This is a basic premise of all forms of personal development, including the development of people skills. Make sure you give it the attention it deserves.

Write Detailed Goals

For the same reason, when you write down a goal make sure you do so in as much detail as possible. If your goals seem sketchy in your own mind, there must be some assertively curious questions you still need to ask. Instead of writing "I want to be given more responsibility in my company," write "I want to become the director of human resources within the next five years, so that I can increase the diversity of our workforce." Once again, you're giving the subconscious mind a detailed set of instructions to work on. The more information you give it, the clearer the final outcome becomes. The more precise the outcome, the more efficient the subconscious mind can be. In this sense, the mind is just like a company. It needs a good business plan before it can act efficiently. Your list of goals is simply a business for your mind to invest in and work toward. If you can actually see the goal you want to achieve when you close your eyes, your heart and your soul can "see" it too.

Suppose you were asked to write down the largest amount of money you feel you can earn in the next twelve months. When you start to do this, maybe some very large figures pop into your mind; figures that seem very unrealistic. You might think, "I can make a million dollars, or two million dollars." But it's too scary, so you won't write it.

What does this tell you? If you're frightened of even writing down the number, consider how much more frightened you must be of actually making this happen. Your reluctance and the difficulty you are having are indications that there's real truth in the seemingly outlandish numbers that entered your mind. Even though they're not based on any material circumstances at the present time, they don't have to be based on physical circumstances. Your thoughts, after all, are the start, and the real start of anything is not based on physical circumstances. When the first airplane flew, was it in the air over Kitty Hawk, North Carolina, or in the minds of the Wright brothers?

Gaining Victory over the Imaginary Observer

Here's the real difficulty that people encounter when they're called upon to formulate a specific goal, especially in writing. We may have been told that this is only for ourselves, that no one else will ever see the number, but we don't really believe that! For the vast majority of people, there's an imaginary person looking over their shoulders. That imaginary person sees the number they've written and says, "Are you crazy? You'll never make that much money in a hundred lifetimes!" So we let the imaginary person make the decision for us. We do this without realizing that this is just as much an expression of our imagination as the million dollars or the fifty million dollars that we were tempted to write down! Since it's a negative expression, you're much more ready to believe it. Why is this?

Don't let this imaginary observer make limiting decisions for you. Be aware that the imaginary observer has no more basis in reality than anything in your wildest dreams. The important thing is what you believe, or even what you *want* to believe. Focus your attention on what you desire before you bring in the imaginary spokesman for "reality."

Let's be very clear about this. If you believe that something is possible, even in your wildest dreams, it is a goal worth striving for. The only qualification is that at some primary level you must believe it is possible. You must be able to take it seriously even if you don't imagine that anyone else can. Then, to become a master of people skills, you must be able to engender that power of belief in everyone around you. The ability to move what's in your mind to the minds of others is the real definition of communication.

In the next chapter we'll move from asking the right questions to sharing the best answers. Our focus will shift from assertive curiosity to assertive communication.

ACTION STEPS

1. Frequent contact is a key to the success of you and your team. Do you have weekly meetings set up with both your subordinates and your superiors? If not, take some time to do so, perhaps creating a memo for those involved, including proposed meeting dates/times, and what you intend to accomplish in them.

2. Many of us are often more negative than we realize. We may spend a great deal of time and energy stating what we "don't want" in our lives instead of what we do want. For one day, take note of every time that you voice something

that you don't want in your life. Make note of both verbal complaints as well as those within your mind. Once you note this tendency, take a moment to state the opposite (what you do want) in the affirmative. Make note of any changes that you experience in your life as you continue to practice this exercise.

3. Take a large sheet of paper and give yourself permission to think big as you list your greatest desires. Write down each and every idea that you get, without filtering anything out of the brainstorm. Then take some time to write those desires out into goals, setting action steps, timelines, and desired outcomes. Finally, for five minutes per day for at least twenty-one days, imagine these goals coming to fruition. Feel into the experiences and give yourself total permission to enjoy the experience fully!

ACTION PLAN NOTES

Any fool can criticize, condemn, and complain—and most fools do.

—Dale Carnegie

CHAPTER 7

From Curiosity to Understanding

We live in a society that values communication skills very highly. We've also become quite sophisticated about how those skills can express themselves. We like people who are able to express themselves well, but we also realize that there's more than one way to do that. Ronald Reagan was known as the Great Communicator, but President Barack Obama is also an outstanding communicator, with a style that's different from Reagan's—or anyone else's.

In light of this, is it possible to draw any general conclusions about what good communicating really involves? Yes and no. There are certain principles that underlie all effective communication, but there's an almost infinite number of ways those principles can be applied. In fact, there are just about as many ways to apply the principles as there are people to apply them.

If you're in a position of leadership and responsibility, knowing how to deal with people is as important as technical or administrative knowledge. Effective managers are part workers and part diplomats. They understand that working with others takes a certain touch, and they hold true to the words of Dale Carnegie: "When dealing with people, remember you are not dealing with creatures of logic, but with creatures of emotion, creatures bristling with prejudice, and motivated by pride and vanity."

Here are some of the cardinal rules of communication in the workplace. In order to master them truly, you have to internalize them and make them part of you. Faking the process will not get you very far.

Call people by name. It's the sweetest sound to anyone's ears. When you use a person's name, you personalize your message; it becomes their own. It also communicates that you care and that you find the person memorable. It's a deceptively simple tool to lower people's guards, since it establishes a bond. Pepper your sentences with names, and start questions with them: "Steve, how are you doing today?"

Admit when you're wrong. You may think that you're losing face if you own up to a mistake. You're not. Recognizing one's own errors is one of the workplace's most honorable acts, since so few people do so. Learn how to put your ego aside and admit that you aren't perfect. Just don't overdo it in an "I blew it" email to the whole office or by gushing apologies at a meeting. A simple "I made a mistake and I realize it" is all that's required.

Hold people to high standards. A certain number of people, commonly labeled "control freaks," seem to think that no one but themselves can do things competently. Don't be one of these people. Trust the abilities of others. In fact, trust them to do the best job possible. It's not about having excessively high expectations. Believing in a person encourages him to do his best not to disappoint. At the same time, be patient with those still getting a handle on a new task.

Show sincere interest. Everyone you meet has a rich history of interests and experiences. Find out about those around you, even if you think you have nothing in common. If a colleague says he likes online game competitions, ask him about it. Really try to understand the reasons why. When you express sincere curiosity, not only will you learn something new but it will take little effort to remember that which you have learned. People like being remembered.

Offer praise. Don't just say "Good job." Be specific in your praise and show that you're aware of what the other person actually did. "You steered that meeting very well, Mike, especially when everyone was distracted" is a good example. At the same time, be sparse with criticism. When it is necessary to coach or provide constructive feedback, do so in a diplomatic and tactful way. We'll have more to say about this later in the chapter.

Keep your word. Don't say you'll do something if you have no intention of following through. Your credibility hangs heavily on your word. If you flake on your promises, you won't be entrusted with critical tasks, and you won't be likely to go far in your career.

Show your gratitude. If someone does you a favor or goes out of their way to get something done for you, make sure you recognize their efforts. You're not automatically entitled to favors, and nobody owes you their extra mile. If you receive one, thank the person and offer to do something in return.

Be considerate. Never assume people will take your words at face value. Some will naturally comb every word a person says, looking for a personal affront. You can't change these people, but when you're around them, you can structure your sentences carefully. Think before you talk and make sure there are no ambiguities that could be misinterpreted.

By making the effort to understand others' points of view, you preclude misunderstandings. You may deeply believe that you are right, but realize that others think the same way about their ideas and beliefs. You have to respect their opinions and see why they think the way they do. Instead of arguing, ask others to explain their positions. You don't have to agree, but you can say "I understand where you're coming from."

Give of yourself. Step out of your job description once in a while and help others with their tasks. Do this without having to be asked. Saying "Need a hand there?" has a twofold effect. First, you encourage others to give of themselves, creating a more positive workplace. Second, you buy yourself a future favor, since kindness always comes back.

Be humble. Obvious efforts to impress your colleagues and superiors will do just the opposite. No one likes a show-off. If you're aching to have your accomplishments acknowledged, you'll simply have to exercise patience. Your achievements will gain genuine approval if you let people discover them instead of flashing it in their faces. And if you play down your successes, you'll be even more respected for your humility.

Help others save face. Everyone makes blunders. Think back to the last time you made an embarrassing gaffe. Didn't you wish someone would step up and play down the seriousness of it? Then do the same for others. Laugh off the faux pas with the person (not at him) with a friendly slap on the shoulder: "It happens to the best of us." Reassure him and others it's not the end of the world. If it's appropriate, say nothing instead of bringing needless attention to the mistake.

FIRST THINGS FIRST

If we consider situations in which communication skills are obviously very important, certain instances immediately come to mind. For example, when you meet someone for the first time, you naturally want to communicate a positive impression. Are you moving into a new role in your company? Perhaps you're changing careers altogether and you're about to meet a new group of colleagues for the first time. Or you may just be at a social event in which you're called upon to introduce yourself to some potential new friends. No matter what the situation, a good first impression is essential if you want to get off on the right foot.

WHEN THE "NEW BROOM" IS YOU

In a workplace setting, you'll usually have an opportunity to introduce yourself to individual team members as well as to the group. It's generally a good idea to meet with everyone both individually and in a more formal group setting.

If you're in a new managerial position, be aware that the change may be destabilizing for the people you'll now be supervising. There may be suspicion that you'll totally change the way things have been working—and this may even be the truth. It's like having a stranger walk into your home and start rearranging the furniture. You are authorized to be in charge, but there are right and wrong ways of doing things.

Start by letting your team know you are open to feedback and suggestions at all times. It is also a good idea to find out what kind of team or sales training has been given up until this point. By discovering what your team already knows and does, you can move forward with more confidence and knowledge.

It is perfectly understandable that any new manager or leader wants to make their own mark. But if you undertake this without seeing how things have been done in the past, you could end up making a very weak first impression. You only get one chance at this. That's why it can pay dividends to give plenty of time to see how the team works before you make any alterations. Get to know people and see how they do things. They might already have great ideas for changes you haven't thought of.

Having spent time getting to know people, you can then follow up with your own expectations for how you see the team working together. Remember that you may be taking over from someone who had a very different leadership style. Whatever you can do to streamline this process will be of great benefit. So pay attention to your first impression. You only get one shot at it.

Here are some final tips for providing constructive feedback:

- *Answer the question "When?"* Effective feedback is sensitive to time, place, and situation. Prepare what you plan to say in advance, tagging specific issues with exactly what you plan to say. Precede your comments with a "heads-up" that feedback is coming, so no one is caught off guard.

- *Answer the question "Where?"* Give feedback privately if possible.

- *Answer the question "What?"* The content of the feedback and how it is delivered are critical elements. Feedback especially should be constructive and targeted. Focus on one area to improve at a time. Genuinely constructive feedback is clear, objective, and specific. Avoid general comments. Focus on skills or practices that are within the person's control. Be descriptive rather than judgmental. Avoid using extreme words like *always* and *never*. Negative feedback is never easy to give, but combining criticism with praise always makes feedback more effective.

- *Answer the question "Who?"* Give feedback on an individual basis, and always allow the team member an opportunity to respond. Good communication is never a one-way street. If people feel the need to defend themselves or explain their actions, definitely allow them to do so. Then work together to find a joint solution.

- *Know how to ask for feedback, and know how to give it in return.* The giving and receiving of an honest response is a key communication skill. One very useful approach to this is known as C-R-C, or "Commend, Recommend, Commend." First you give a sincere compliment, then follow with practical suggestions for improvement, and close with further praise. At each step, the key is empathy and sincerity.

When dealing with any interpersonal communication, always be aware that what you believe to be the truth is a subjective issue. What you may find ineffective, inappropriate, or even distasteful may be perfectly acceptable or desirable from another person's point of view. That's why it's important to leaven whatever constructive feedback you give with a generous helping of sincere praise. Remember that the attitude of the speaker influences the attitude of the listener, which in turn leads to action on the part of both of them.

MAKE YOURSELF CLEAR

If you've attended a conference or lecture recently, you're aware that people are usually asked to turn off their cell phones before the first speaker begins. But what would happen if, instead of being asked to turn off their phones, the audience was asked to put their ring tones on high volume? Almost certainly, there would be an annoying intrusion every few minutes. In fact, there would probably be many of them at the same time.

Something very much like this is actually happening every time you're in conversation with another person. You may not hear it, but several times a minute that person's "mental cell phone" is ringing—and there may be times when the person even answers the call and has a whole internal conversation. You don't even know it, because you've just gone on talking. You've probably done the same thing too. It seemed like you were listening to the person sitting across from you, but you were really listening to someone else entirely.

The human mind can receive only a certain amount of information at any given moment. In one form or another—whether they're sights, sounds, or mental images—messages are coming in at every second of the day. To get someone's complete attention in the midst of this bombardment, your communication must be clear, direct, and to the point. Here are some pointers for making that happen:

Take your time. Every person is different, yet people in general are surprisingly the same. Each of us is both a type and an individual, with at least as many similarities as differences. To communicate effectively, the first requirement is knowing which qualities you share with another person and which ones separate you—and this takes some time. Too many people simply assume that they know all they need to know about another human being. They just start talking. If you have something important to say to a new acquaintance—whether it's a recent hire in your department or the new coach of your daughter's soccer team—don't assume you already know everything you need to know about this person. That's especially true when you're in a leadership role, such as department head or sales manager.

Be frank about what you need. This is very important in both professional and personal communication. You need to be assertive but not aggressive, frank but not blunt. Suppose, for example, that you feel it's time to ask for a raise. That's a request that raises some delicate communication issues that you'll need to handle correctly. It's not just a matter of walking into your supervisor's office and blurting out your desire (or even your need) for more money. This should be approached with respect and planning, and it should begin long before you actually make the request. Weeks or even months before you meet with the decision maker, you should begin building your case.

Create a paper trail. As you build a case, a good place to start is by keeping a written record of every assignment you have completed for your employer, whether it was menial or monumental. If you were smart, you should have been maintaining a job log from the outset. The milestones you have completed will document your request for a higher salary. Basically, you are asking your employer to increase his costs, and you've got to offer a compelling justification for that.

Think of yourself as an attorney presenting an argument in front of a judge and jury. You have to build a case in order to win a favorable decision for your client—but now your client happens to be yourself. Your employer won't take your request seriously if you don't treat it seriously. So put in a considerable amount of effort and time in order to prepare for your inquiry. Don't overlook anything. Did you come up with an idea that saved the firm thousands of dollars last year? That's great, but don't forget how you also dressed up like Santa Claus for the company Christmas party, and find a way to work that into the conversation.

Regardless of the data you offer in support of your request, the manner in which you present your case is just as important. This is where clarity and calm are so important. No matter what the outcome of your raise request, maintain a sense of dignity and professional pride. If you do in fact have a legitimate request, you will get what you deserve, whether now or a bit further down the road.

In more personal conversations, documentation is much less important than directness and sincerity. Most people really don't want to hear about the history of their relationships. They don't want you to recount what was said at Thanksgiving two years ago or promises that were made on the beach at sunset. It's much more effective to focus on the present and the future. But one thing is always true no matter who you're talking to or for what purpose: You must have identified your needs in your own mind, and you must be able to state them clearly. If you get turned down, you know you gave it your best shot. But if you really give it your best shot, the chances are you won't get turned down.

TO RESOLVE CONFLICTS, BRING THEM TO THE SURFACE

Not many of us are born knowing how to handle conflict. It takes years of practice, and the practice can be painful. But the first step to conflict resolution is full disclosure. Your employees or even your spouse might be harboring resentments toward you. Once these dark secrets are brought into the light of day, how should you proceed?

Stay calm. It might be tempting to let off steam or pull rank. But once you become angry, it is easy to lose focus and become more interested in the battle than in a positive outcome. If you want to handle conflict effectively, you need to be fully composed.

Encourage communication. Silence may be golden, but silence is unlikely to move things forward when there's conflict. It's essential to encourage verbal communication, and the best way to do that is with attentive listening.

Focus on a win-win outcome. When starting from a place of conflict, chances are that the initial prognosis will be win-lose. At that point, it's just a question of who will come out on top. The win-win option, on the other hand, is a solution that all parties can commit to without feeling anyone has lost. Finding that solution begins with belief that it really exists and that it is possible to achieve. This is why you need to be able to motivate your team if you want to create a productive work environment. By combining good motivational practices with meaningful work, the setting of performance goals, and use of an effective reward system, you can establish the kind of atmosphere and culture that you need in order to excel. The better you are able to link these factors together, the higher the motivation levels of your team are likely to be. That's a win-win for you, for them, and for your organization.

Set the ground rules. When people are locking horns, it is important to set some ground rules or agreements around what is acceptable in terms of resolving the issues. These ground rules need to be agreed on collectively rather than being imposed by anyone—even you.

Respond, don't react. When someone "vents" on you, the challenge is to maintain your poise and your patience. Don't reflexively go into a defensive posture. Give the other person an opportunity to express their concerns, and even their anger, fully.

When you do this without becoming reactive, you gain tremendous power in the exchange—because the person who gets angry alone is always the loser. As an interpersonal tactic, anger works only if both parties buy into it. If you refuse to play that game, you're the automatic winner. So have the courage it takes to look at the truth without fear or blame—because the truth will set you free.

PRAISE: THE SECRET WEAPON

In many corporate cultures, overt praise is in short supply, because most people don't know how to deliver it well. When given only as an attempt to please others or to qualify oneself, flattery is indeed lame. But delivered wisely and subtly—insightfully, specifically, and empathetically—praise can do wonders.

The truth is, nothing is more potent in human communication than a well-placed compliment, but very few people know how to take advantage of this fact. The cardinal rule of flattery is that it should be insightful, specific, and empathetic. That means no generic brown-nosing. It means actually noticing something that the other guy may be unaware of. Take these steps to distinguish your praise from mere lip service.

Give specific compliments. Understand what makes people nervous, and focus on paying compliments that will comfort them regarding that. For a business leader, it may be addressing and inspiring a crowd of subordinates. For an assistant, it may be her knowledge of office protocol. For a writer, it's likely his way with words. You need to pay attention to where a person's lack of confidence lies. Then compliment them accordingly, in the most natural way possible.

Time your praise. Giving praise and showing appreciation is usually most effective immediately after someone does something they deserve praise for. It's directly after the fact that most people are nervous and itching to hear that they did well. Let time pass and they will calm down or convince themselves that they did well and don't need anyone else's approval. Timing also involves assessing someone's mood. If you see a coworker in a slump, a well-placed and sincere compliment might motivate him and remind him that his work is really important.

Keep praise professional. In a business setting, limit your compliments to work-related achievements, since that is a person's main function in the office. Complimenting someone on a good joke they sent around by email doesn't count.

Praise your boss carefully. Complimenting managers demands tact. In general, this is better as an aside than directly. Praise your boss to others. You can also use office gossip to your advantage. Speak highly of your boss to others in the office. Tell them how pleasant it is to work for this person (only if it's true, of course!). The reliable grapevine will transmit your words to the chief in no time. For the truly tactical, a good way to compliment managers is to learn about their interests and engage in conversation about them. Few people expect others to enjoy their own tastes. Doing so can be very flattering.

Compliments should be valuable. Why is platinum expensive? Because there's a scarce amount of it out there. Your compliments should remain rare if they are to have any effect. Overdo it and people will not only come to expect your flattery but they'll be unaffected by it. Compliments are also more valuable if they're honest. You need to develop a reputation for tactful honesty. Once you're a trusted source of information, your compliments go much further.

MAKE CHANGES WHEN RELATIONSHIPS BECOME UNPRODUCTIVE

In closing, let's face the fact that sometimes you need to walk away from a relationship that has become overwhelmingly toxic. But that drastic step usually can be prevented by less drastic adjustments. If you're worried about how a meeting may turn out, for example, it might be a good idea to meet in a neutral location off-site rather than in the boss's office or a conference room. Sometimes it means moving the meeting from right after lunch to first thing next morning, when clearer heads might prevail. It might also mean your level of assertiveness to ensure your point is being received. Sometimes it might mean bringing others into the meeting so that the other person understands the results of their attitudes or actions.

And if all else fails, be prepared to move on.

ACTION STEPS

Many of the principles Dale Carnegie writes about in *How to Win Friends and Influence People* apply directly to communication. Circle the one principle that presents the biggest challenge to you personally and make a commitment to begin applying this immediately. Record the benefits received as a result of this new approach.

- To get the best of an argument—avoid it.

- Show respect for the other person's opinion. Never tell a person he or she is wrong.

- If you are wrong, admit it quickly, emphatically.

- Begin in a friendly way. Get the other person saying yes immediately.

- Let the other person do a great deal of the talking.

- Let the other person feel the idea is his or hers.

- Try honestly to see things from the other person's point of view.

- Be sympathetic to the other person's ideas and desires.

- Appeal to nobler motives.

- Dramatize your ideas.

- Speak softly.

- Maintain open body language.

- Sustain soft eye contact.

- Smile appropriately.

- Maintain an appropriate physical distance.

- Keep posture attentive; lean forward slightly.

- Don't interrupt.

- And if a confrontation can't be avoided, don't feel you have to get an unconditional surrender. Always give the other person an opening for an honorable retreat.

ACTION PLAN NOTES

Instead of worrying about what people say of you, why not spend time trying to accomplish something they will admire.

—Dale Carnegie

CHAPTER 8

Etiquette: Rules of the Road for People Skills

E tiquette is really just another word for manners, and manners is really shorthand for people skills. Etiquette is a "do unto others" system of actions and reactions, and is every bit as applicable in today's urban environments as it was in earlier settings. Living in a big city can be great, but learning the unwritten rules of city living takes time and careful observation. Just as in the country, if you're polite and respectful, chances are that others will be polite and respectful right back at you. However, if you're not mindful of the basic rules of urban etiquette, you'll likely get some very nasty glares.

In this chapter we'll look at some of the settings and issues that require a working knowledge of contemporary etiquette. Some of them may surprise you. You may not have realized that everyday occurrences such as conversation or going out for coffee are actually governed by "rules of the road," but by the end of this chapter you should be able to pass your driver's test and get your license. Just pay close attention to what follows.

CONVERSATIONAL ETIQUETTE

What's fair game to discuss in a conversation? The answer might be "anything is fair game," provided you're talking with friends or family members. But what about interactions with colleagues and coworkers? Here you have to be a little more careful.

A safe nonbusiness topic is one that won't provoke an unnecessary amount of debate or any hostility to speak of. Among business professionals, popular chatter topics includes sports, current events, your personal background, and of course your work. If you're doing business anyway, then talking about work can be useful, but people will find a little bit of variety refreshing. If you do talk about your career, just make sure that it doesn't turn into gossip about your boss or colleagues—unless you have something really nice to say about them!

Just like a personal conversation, a good business interaction needs flow to stay healthy. Perhaps you're a person who really likes to talk. That's fine when you're just being social, but to someone who doesn't know you that well, this can be irritating in a business situation. But it gets worse. What about a person who dominates a conversation without even realizing it? It's like bad breath: even your best friends won't tell you.

You can avoid these traps by using a time limit designed to keep you from babbling incessantly. If you're asked a question, keep your answer to less than sixty seconds long. But don't just mutter a few words either. The goal is to keep a steady flow and encourage attentiveness in your companions. For a telephone conversation, being attentive is vitally important since you can't see the person you're speaking to. That makes it difficult to gauge the level of attention. When you're not talking, let the other person finish their thought without your jumping in and trying to finish it for them. When it's your turn to speak, you hope they'll grant you the same courtesy.

Just as you would treat your conversation partner with respect, make sure you treat everyone else in their company the same way. That includes everyone from their colleagues at a business event to their assistants on the phone. Equal respect across the board makes your sincerity clearly visible. There's also a very pragmatic reason for this. It will help your chances of getting through to a senior manager when the person redirecting your call to a key business contact has a positive association with you.

LISTEN CAREFULLY

Listening takes practice, because everybody wants to talk. It's like stopping at a traffic light or paying your income tax: Listening may not be something you initially want to do, but you can come to an understanding that it's necessary for the greater good. If you can avoid talking as much as a sports announcer or a game-show host, it's a snap to listen like a pro. Listening will help you get to know the person you're talking to and work toward creating a solid bond, which will be a building block toward a healthy and ongoing business relationship. If you can lay off the urge to talk too much and listen respectfully, your own words will count for more by coming through louder and clearer at the appropriate times.

Beyond the basic act of listening, the next step is to let the other party *know* that you're listening—also known as active listening. If you're talking in person, you can use body language—eye contact, head nodding—in response to what they say. Try always to add brief remarks that address their points and show an appreciation and understanding for what they're saying. Think of it as your way of sharing your understanding and attention level with the person talking.

Listening gets a bit more difficult if the person you're listening to doesn't have very much to say. Sure, you can politely walk away or hang up and cut your losses, but sometimes people want to open up. You can encourage them by asking a lot of open-ended questions and using keywords that hint at your interest in a topic and a desire to hear further details. It could be as easy as saying something like "I'm new to promotions. It sounds interesting. I'd like to learn more" to a promotions director from your company's trade partner. When you do this, it makes them feel comfortable and confident in what they're discussing and they'll be more willing to open up. But once you've got your listening skills down, you're all set.

CONVERSATION ETIQUETTE MISTAKES

The way you talk to others goes a long way toward *establishing your credibility* or losing it in an instant. Where conversation is concerned, the worst of the worst blunders are inappropriate topics, office gossip, interrupting, and raising your voice.

You might feel targeted if a boss or client is angry with you, but you'll make it worse by interrupting and raising your voice. Shouting and interrupting aren't suitable with *coworkers* either. Yelling across the office to start a conversation is distracting and embarrassing, while interrupting another conversation to "join in" shows impatience and lack of respect.

CONVERSATION ETIQUETTE TIPS

Aim small with your conversations and don't go out-of-bounds. Asking basic questions and paying attention will lead to common ground and steer you away from taboos. Keep your personal life private and don't be a gossip. Instead of talking about others, pay respectful compliments to them instead. If they do the same for you, always thank them. You won't regret it.

Regrets can't be undone after a testy argument, so when dealing with an irate client or manager, be proactive and problem-solve. Instead of interrupting or yelling, hear them out and don't judge. Think about their main issue and calmly offer some solutions. You'd probably be just as upset if you were in their situation, so imagine how you would want to be treated. Also be considerate when starting coworker conversations. Try walking over to see them and if they're busy, come back or leave a voice mail.

THE TRADE-OFF

With professional power comes professional responsibility. The ability to work well in your career is a must, but being able to conduct yourself continually in a professional manner is equally critical. One embarrassing miscue could send you packing in a hurry.

The ever-expanding rule book of professional etiquette can make it hard to keep up, but the following business blunders are universally condemned. Here's how to spot them and what you can do to stay in the safe zone.

Using profanity, intruding on personal space, and unnecessary cell phone chats top the list of behavioral blunders. (By the way, transgressions of etiquette aren't good anywhere, but they're most harmful at work, where people witness them up close and on a regular basis.)

Don't use profanity to make a point. It'll take away your credibility and make you look childish. In addition to profanity, standing too close to a coworker or being physical with them is also unwise. The work environment isn't a place for intimacy.

Although an office setting favors speech over intimacy, that shouldn't include your cell phone. A sudden call at a meeting or lunch can be irritating, especially if you're talking loudly. Even a loud ring tone shouldn't be allowed to happen.

Always choose humor over profanity, as it will keep the attention on you and you'll be well liked for your efforts. When you're humoring or even just interacting with someone, give them a respectable distance of fifteen inches, smile often, and acknowledge them, as a sign of respect.

Cell phone talk can be lessened through caller ID screening and voice mail, as most calls are unnecessary. Anticipate potential callers and call them first—before work. Don't answer in a meeting, and speak quietly if you really must take a call. Don't make your phone visible on a desk or a lunch table.

MONEY ETIQUETTE

Business is all about money, isn't it? Actually, no. Business is about a lot more than money. It's about people, and money is an important vehicle for conveying your relationships with the people you work with. In fact, personal money issues come up all the time in the workplace and it will be to your great benefit if you know how to handle them. Instead of speaking theoretically about issues of money etiquette, let's look at a number of real-life situations and see how they're best handled. Some of these examples are clearly work related, some clearly are not, and some seem to split the difference. But money is always money, so it's best to be prepared.

Someone takes you out for a meal at a nice restaurant but leaves a very small tip. The service wasn't great, but not bad either. Can you add cash to the table?

It depends on whom you're with. If your host is a close friend or relative, you can say, "Would you mind if I put down a few dollars? You probably didn't notice, but our server was extra helpful to me." With someone you don't know well, however, it's better to just let it go. You wouldn't want to seem like an ungrateful or judgmental guest.

Your coworkers are collecting money for someone's baby gift. You are new to the company and don't really know the recipient. Do you have to contribute as much as the senior staff?

Not at all. Chip in what you can, and a few dollars is fine. Office celebrations can be so frequent that contributing might get burdensome. One solution—suggest that your group try a collection pool. Pick a month to start and have everyone contribute an agreed-upon amount. The resulting fund pays for parties and gifts for the next year. No more collections, no more pressure.

Your daughter often asks you to sponsor her school in book drives or other charitable events. You don't let your own kids collect from relatives nearly this often. How do you stop the cycle?

Just say no. You've become your daughter's best customer—why would she stop soliciting for more? The next time she asks, let her know that you'll be cutting back: "Danielle, I'll be happy to participate, but you should know that this is the only fund-raiser that I can give to this year." It's never too early to learn the difference between a benefactor and an ATM machine.

You live on a cul-de-sac that ends in a large grass-covered patch, which the neighbors take turns mowing all summer. Now some people (including you) want to hire a lawn service, but others are balking at the cost. What now?

Unless you have a neighborhood association where the majority rules, you can't force dissenters to pay. Instead, graciously accept everyone's decision, then designate which weeks the service will mow and which weeks the nonpaying households will take their turns.

Your department head is having a milestone birthday, so you and three of your junior colleagues are chipping in for a group gift. Should the cost be divided evenly? Or should you, as the senior person who is more highly paid, put in more?

The cost should be split four ways. The numbers are probably not so high that anyone will be seriously damaged—and it might even be insulting to suggest that a coworker could not afford to contribute an equal share.

PHONE ETIQUETTE

A number of commentators have pointed out that more business is lost because of poor phone communication than for any other reason. The telephone is a very precarious medium. Some of the reasons for this are obvious. When you're talking on the phone you have no idea what the other party might be doing, even though you believe you're getting his or her full attention. In fact, you don't even know who else might be in the room. So be aware of both the importance and the perils of telephone communication. The following guidelines will help.

Always return calls within twenty-four hours. This should be your rule for all phone calls, but especially for business communications. Even if you don't yet have an answer to the caller's question, call and explain what you're doing to get the requested information, or direct them to the appropriate place to get it.

If you're going to be out or unavailable at work, have someone pick up your calls or, at a minimum, have your answering system tell the caller when you'll be back in the office and when they can expect a call back.

When you initiate a call and get a receptionist or secretary, identify yourself and clarify the basic nature of your call. That way you'll be sure you're getting the right person or department, and the person you're trying to reach will be able to pull up the appropriate information and help you more efficiently.

When you're on the receiving end of a phone call, identify yourself and your department. Answer the phone with some enthusiasm or at least very politely. Even if you are being interrupted, the person on the other end doesn't know that!

Make sure your voice-mail system is working properly and doesn't tell the caller that the mailbox is full, transfer them to nowhere, or ring indefinitely. Address technical and system problems. A rude machine or system is as unacceptable as a rude person.

You don't have to reply to obvious telemarketers. If someone is calling to sell you something, you can indicate that you are not interested and hang up without losing too much time on it. However, you do need to be careful. You may be receiving a call from an insurance or long distance company that wants to hire you as a consultant! Be sure you know the nature of the call before you (politely, of course) excuse yourself.

Personalize the conversation. Many people interact via electronic media the way they behave in their cars. They feel that since they're not face-to-face with a person, it is perfectly acceptable to be abrupt, crass, or rude. We need to ensure that we make best use of the advantages of these mediums without falling headfirst into the disadvantages.

RESTAURANT ETIQUETTE

Going out to eat with a group of friends or colleagues should be a pleasant social experience. Toward that end, it's important to deal with the money issues discreetly and gracefully. In a time of tightened budgets, the sometimes significant costs of dining out can't be ignored. That doesn't mean you always have to grab the check, but don't pretend that it doesn't exist either.

Make it clear if you're treating. You can invite friends to a restaurant without picking up the tab, but use language that makes it clear. Say, "John, would you and Ellen like to meet us at Jackson's Grill on Saturday? If you're up for it, I'll make the reservation." If you do want to pay for everyone's dinner, you'd phrase it differently: "We're hosting a dinner and would like you to be our guests." A written invitation also says that you are treating.

Avoid haggling. When you go out to dinner with a group of people, you should assume that the check will be split equally rather than calculated down to the penny. It's easiest for everyone, so plan accordingly. But if you think you'll be ordering just a light salad with no cocktails and want to pay appropriately, ask for separate bills before you order. (Most restaurants will comply.) Or, when plans are being made, say, "I'd really like to come, but I'm strapped for cash this month. I hope you won't mind if I get a separate bill." You won't overpay, and the arrangement doesn't have to be discussed at the table.

Don't skip tips. If your experience was less than wonderful, it's okay to leave 10 percent or even 8 percent if the service was genuinely rude. But leaving nothing is harsh as well as ambiguous—the server may think you forgot. Decide if the waiter really caused the problems (it might have been the kitchen's fault that the food was so slow in coming out). And don't wait until you're leaving to express dissatisfaction. Mention it as soon as you can so the waiter has a chance to make a positive change.

Leave a tip for the bartender. Always tip a bartender—usually a $1 minimum, unless the service was terrible. Waiters and bartenders survive on tips. If you can afford to eat out, you can afford to tip.

Tip beforehand. Tip the coat check employee and the valet at the beginning of the night. Regardless of what you earn, don't cheap out on tipping the people who serve you.

Ladies first. In a mixed group, women should always be allowed to pick their seat of preference. A man should gesture for them to take their seat first; then, after they've started to sit down, he may do so also. Similarly, women should always order first. Most waiters should instinctively begin with the woman—but if they don't, men should offer to let their female companions choose first. The days of chivalry may be dead, but the desire to be treated with respect is as alive today as it was in the past.

Keep a lid on it. Don't have drawn-out conversations on your cell phone in a restaurant. If you must, simply answer and tell the caller that you will call them back at a later time if it's not urgent. Better yet, turn off your phone or put it on vibrate or silent mode. A simple rule of thumb should be that people come before electronics. Cell phones should also be turned off in movie theaters, at concerts, during plays, and at any other time when taking a call will disturb the patrons around you.

The clock is always ticking. When you're speaking with a wait-person or with a cashier, a certain amount of friendly banter is appropriate. After all, it's important to acknowledge the existence of these people as human beings and not as mere servants. But don't start gabbing as if no one else were waiting to be taken care of.

ETIQUETTE IN A NUTSHELL

Most behavior that is perceived as disrespectful, discourteous, or abrasive is unintentional. It could have been avoided by practicing good etiquette. Basic knowledge and practice of etiquette is a valuable advantage, because in a lot of situations, a second chance may not be practical or even possible.

The most important thing to remember is to be courteous and thoughtful to the people around you, regardless of the situation. Consider other people's feelings and stick to your convictions as diplomatically as possible. Address conflict as situation-related, rather than person-related. Apologize when you step on toes. You can't go too far wrong if you stick with the basics you learned (or were supposed to learn) in kindergarten—not that those basics are always easy to remember when you're in a crucial business meeting.

Along these lines, the qualities we admire most in adults are the very traits we work so hard to engender in our children. If you always behave so that you would not mind if your spouse, kids, or grandparents were watching you, you're probably doing fine. Avoid raising your voice, using harsh or derogatory language toward anyone, or interrupting. In a business setting, you may not get as much "airtime" in meetings at first, but what you do say will be much more effective because it carries the weight of cred-ibility and respectability.

IT'S ABOUT PEOPLE

While at work, talk and visit with the people around you. Don't differentiate among them by position or standing within the company. The next time you need a document prepared or a conference room arranged for a presentation, watch how many people are involved with that process (you'll probably be surprised!) and make it a point to meet them and show your appreciation.

Make it a point to arrive ten or fifteen minutes early and visit with people who work near you. When you're visiting another site, linger over a cup of coffee and introduce yourself to people nearby. If you arrive early for a meeting, introduce yourself to the other participants. At social occasions, use the circumstances of the event itself as an icebreaker. After introducing yourself, ask how they know the host or how they like the crab dip. Talk a little about yourself—your hobbies, kids, or pets; just enough to get people to open up about theirs and get to know you as a person.

Try to remember everything you can about as many people as possible. Then use this information in thoughtful ways. Send cards or letters for birthdays or congratulations of promotions or other events; send flowers for engagements and weddings or in condolence for the death of a loved one or family member. People will remember your kindness, probably much longer than you will!

ACTION STEPS

What messages are you sending by your actions, words, and attitudes? Ask yourself whether you've done any of the following:

- Conducted personal business on company time?

- Used or taken company resources for personal purposes?

- Called in sick when you weren't sick?

- Engaged in negative gossip or spread rumors about someone?

- Passed on information that had been shared in confidence?

- Knowingly violated company rules or procedures?

- Failed to follow through on something you said you would do?

- Withheld information that others needed?

- Fudged on a time sheet, invoice, or expense account?

- Knowingly delivered second-rate goods or services?

- Been less than honest in order to make a sale?

- Accepted an inappropriate gift or gratuity?

- Taken or accepted credit for something that someone else did?

- Failed to admit to or correct a mistake? Or knowingly let someone else make a mistake and get into trouble?

These and other seemingly minor actions reflect who you are and what you stand for. When it comes to etiquette, everything is important—especially "the small stuff." In your action plan, make clear notes of ways you can improve in this area, and then diligently follow up in your work and in your personal relationships.

ACTION PLAN NOTES

One of the surest ways of making a friend and influencing the opinion of another is to give consideration to his opinion, to let him sustain his feeling of importance.

—Dale Carnegie

CHAPTER 9

Persuasion as a People Skill

Suppose you could get anyone to do whatever you wanted. It's actually not that difficult. Some people devote their lives to mastering the art of persuasion, but the basic methods are quite straightforward.

Persuasion is a very specific people skill. Basically, it's getting people onto your side of the fence without the use of force or intimidation. It's convincing others to internalize your argument, then embrace it as a part of their own belief system.

IDENTIFYING A NEED

Attempting to persuade others to believe you when you lack an identifiable urgency is pointless. If the thing you want—support, money, approval—isn't obvious, you'll need to make it obvious by demonstrating a profound need and energizing it with enthusiasm, evidence, and urgency.

In order to get your audience on your side, you have to convince them of a need they may not be aware they had. For example, you need to get a program off the ground immediately because now is the only time it can be implemented with the best possible results.

Toward the goal of persuading their listeners, people use a variety of "loaded" words. Politicians refer to the "war on terror" and "defending democracy." Advertisers tout a product as "all natural." What exactly does this mean? And how much does it really matter? In the desire to persuade, meaning itself is often secondary when loaded words are used.

Warren Buffett rarely fails to refer to his investors as "partners," though they do not meet this definition. He knows, however, that doing so instills a sense of fraternity and amiability without his having to give up anything at all. It's a simple and effective tactic, because people tend to agree with those who show interest, respect, and even affection. Toward that end, a basic means of persuasion involves not only using words that listeners understand and recognize but even doing something as simple as calling them by name. It's as basic as meeting someone for the first time. If you're able to remember and use their name, you're bound to make a far better impression. This assures the listener that somebody has paid attention to who they actually are. People naturally feel more significant when their names are remembered.

As you begin to understand this, you're on your way to mastering the people skill of persuasion. As components of this skill, three factors are especially powerful.

Authority: A connection to recognized and established authority satisfies a basic need of any listener. People want to feel that you come from a position of legitimate power. This can be done by displaying your own background and mastery in a particular area or by introducing and aligning yourself with the words and work of an individual who is recognized as a master.

Emotion: Too often, people incorrectly assume that the world is concerned only with facts. While numbers have their place and should never be ignored entirely, an appeal to emotions can prove especially effective in a business setting. The key is to evoke an emotional response by using metaphors or appealing to a sense of adventure.

Reason: Appealing to reason involves the application of unimpeachable facts and figures to influence your audience. For many in the business world, this is the best form of persuasion. Linked with emotion, reason and logic convey the impression of authority, if only because you will appear to be extremely well prepared.

PERSUASION, STEP BY STEP

The art of persuasion can be described in terms of a logical, step-by-step progression. It really all boils down to stating your case clearly and effectively. But before you can even begin to do that, you must thoroughly understand your audience—*who* they are and *why* they think the way they do. This gives you two important insights. You can empathize with your listeners, establishing a human connection, and you can construct your arguments to show why your view is the one that will work not just to your benefit but to theirs as well.

Build trust. People are automatically wary of anyone who's trying to change their minds. This is why it's paramount to gain their trust by convincing them that you are sincere and well intentioned. Show them why you should be heard. You must know what you're talking about and prove that there is good reason why you think the way you do.

Find common ground. Many people share similar ideas about what's fair and desirable. Show your audience that your values and ideas mesh with their own. Again, you need to put yourself in their shoes, understand their concerns, and be sympathetic to their feelings.

Structure your information. Any persuasive argument—be it a speech, an essay, or a sales pitch—has a clear structure. Verbally, a successful structure is about repetition and placement. When listing reasons why people should listen to you, save your most powerful points for last, as they will linger in the minds of your captive audience. Also, repeat your most important arguments. Repetition establishes a pattern that remains in the memory.

Show both sides. Weigh the pros and cons of your ideas, as doing so will make you seem fair and reasonable to others. The trick here is to emphasize the pros and underplay the cons. Explain why the cons aren't so bad, or how the benefits outweigh the drawbacks. Never lie about the cons, because if and when people find out about your deception, they'll resent you. And they will never trust you again.

Appeal to self-interest. You are more likely to convince someone of an idea if you show them what they stand to gain from it, as this is a question that will always be at the back of their minds. For this to work, you'll need to know what your audience's needs are. Grab their attention by telling them you know what they want, then tell them how your idea will satisfy that.

Appeal to authority. As mentioned earlier, everyone loves experts. Everyone listens to experts. If an expert says something, it must be true. So use them in your talk. Find out how your idea, or elements of it, has been approved or endorsed by specialists in this area.

Create consensus. Most people are influenced by what others are doing. You need to show that what you want is approved by a large number of people. Use examples of how your ideas are successful elsewhere or how others have enjoyed them. You can also use a kind of reverse consensus: If what most people are doing is undesirable, show them why and convince them about your idea.

Time your request. You need to develop a sixth sense for good timing. Avoid approaching people with requests during times of great stress. Learn to gauge the general mood and how receptive people will be to you. Look for periods of general confidence and high morale. Make others feel safe and self-assured if necessary.

Be original. It's a simple law of economics: The more scarce something is, the higher its price. Make yourself or your ideas seem unique or rare, and people will listen more. You can do this by either demonstrating that you hold exclusive information or suggesting that there's a competitor for what you have to offer.

Be interesting. When you talk in a monotone with lots of *um*'s, you will lose people the second you start talking. You need to be unique and energized, showing that you are excited about your idea. Appeal to their senses as much as you can. If you're making a presentation, use lots of visual and audio aids. An impressive spectacle can be as effective as eloquent sentences.

Be reasonable. People like to think they are reasonable, so appeal to their sense of reason. Logic is highly valued in business, and your words should have a logical format. Use an "if . . . then" argument: "If you do this, then good things will happen."

Be diplomatic. You must treat your audience as you would like to be treated. Speak in a proper tone; don't yell or talk down to them. More importantly, don't make them feel foolish for thinking differently from you. You want to reason with people, not argue with them. Even if you win the argument, they will resent you. You'll gain their respect if you are respectful.

Be humble. No one likes a holier-than-thou egomaniac. Although you believe your idea is better, if you come across as arrogant, people will stop listening. Also, you shouldn't assume you will convince them right away. Be realistic and accept that you may be turned down.

Use persuasion sparingly. It's been said that persuasion is like a savings account: The less you use it, the more you've got. Learn how to use your powers of persuasion well and at the appropriate moments. With time and practice, you'll be able to have positive influence on people's decisions in any number of areas.

PERSUASIVE SALES TECHNIQUES

Every day people are exposed to sales techniques in various aspects of their lives and schedules. For example, while listening to the morning radio or television over breakfast, a number of advertisements will come over the airways during program breaks. On the drive to work, billboards and signs on the sides of buses and vehicles coax viewers to consider certain products. On the job, a coworker may try to convince others to buy Girl Scout cookies to support her daughter's troop. The boss could hint that year-end bonuses will be bigger than ever with a little more effort from employees. At dinner in a favorite restaurant, the menu displays mouthwatering photos of expensive entrees and uses descriptive language to persuade customers to try these items.

Persuasion techniques are everywhere, and they can be powerful. They can be helpful, as when pointing out the best foods for maintaining good health. They also can be harmful in attracting teens to buy provocative clothing or illegal products, like cigarettes or alcoholic beverages. Becoming more aware of persuasion techniques can arm the average consumer with knowledge on how to resist unwanted or unnecessary purchases. A typical sales strategy follows these steps.

- Get the customer's attention.

- Create or identify a need, problem, or desire.

- Offer a solution.

- Close the sale.

Let's look at the first of these four steps. How do persuasive individuals get the attention of busy, apathetic, or resistant people? There are dozens of ways that are used to put into practice one of the steps listed above. To get a better idea of how persuasion is used to grab someone's attention, here are some of the most common strategies and persuasion techniques.

"You need it." A problem is identified, and a solution is offered. This can take the form of a broad issue such as corruption in office during a political campaign: "As a citizen of this state, you need honesty from your government leaders. John Doe is the only honest candidate!"

"You deserve it." A limit, lack, or gap is met with the ability to fill it. One example: "You deserve more leisure time. We offer an affordable weekend getaway package."

"You want it." The persuader arouses a desire and provides a way of meeting it. "Craving chocolate? Try these deliciously rich dark chocolate nuggets." After tasting a sample, the person may be induced to buy more, even when the item is not on the person's grocery list or within their budget.

"Try a sample." Although you will receive a free sample, the hope is to awaken interest in the product and get the potential customer to buy, whether it is a sample of food, pen, new book, et cetera.

"Everyone is counting on you." This persuasion technique is used, for example, to convince someone to buy health products so that they can stay well for their family or to suggest a community connection where every vote counts.

"A onetime opportunity" Many marketers use this persuasive approach to argue that a particular product is available on a limited basis. For example, a new car may sit on the lot for months, but today might be the only time the salesperson is willing to reduce the price by $300 (or whatever amount).

"Quality, not quantity" When shopping for new merchandise, a sales associate will point out that a more expensive item is built better or has more features, even if it costs more.

"Helping others" The thinking behind this strategy is that endorsing a certain product, idea, or individual will actually help the economy, society, or person. For example, buying an American-made car without considering fuel costs will show support for the U.S. economy instead of supporting overseas-made imports.

"Benefits list" A persuasive salesperson can emphasize a host of benefits perhaps several times during the contact, whether in a media advertisement or an in-person sales push. Any negatives or cost will be downplayed to focus on possible positives.

"Win-win" In getting a person to do something, it is implied that both parties will come out ahead. For example, if a customer buys a discounted picture painted by a "starving artist," the customer gets a good deal while the artist makes money and builds a reputation.

"Either-or" Narrowing the choices to an either-or decision puts pressure on the customer and channels the choice in one of two directions. "Either vote this candidate in or expect continued corruption."

"Scare tactics" This approach creates a fear mentality to suggest that failure to do what the speaker wants may result in loss, damage, or destruction.

"Bandwagon approach" The persuader will point out that the smart or popular people are using the product or buying into the idea, with the implication that those who don't are the opposite kind of people.

In assessing persuasive techniques like these, you need to understand the processes that are at work. While a product or idea may hold merits, you as a buyer should be convinced by those merits, not by covering negatives and inflating positives. A thoughtful consumer will think about the pros and cons of adopting an outlook that is pushed by someone and consider the logic of a particular point of view.

Persuasion techniques come in many variations. That's why it's better to avoid making hurried purchases or too quickly adding assent to an issue where facts may be missing or where persuasive strategies like these may color the logic to block wisdom's path.

BODY LANGUAGE: NONVERBAL PERSUASIVENESS

We're all sending silent messages out into the world, and the vocabulary we use consists of a reliable, legible set of motions and gestures. Body language—nonverbal communication—expresses our deeper feelings, even when those feelings contrast with the words we use. Facial expressions, the position of arms and legs and hands, how we sit, stand, listen, and speak all convey differing degrees of deceit or honesty, concern or uninterest. Very simply, a wealth of information.

Some silent communications are casual; others are a chess game. Whether meeting a date or going in front of a boss, learning to decode body language can provide a tremendous advantage. You can decipher what people are truly feeling but, for whatever reason, have chosen not to convey verbally. Often, what goes unspoken can be a tremendous source of insight just waiting to be tapped. Furthermore, understanding nonverbal cues allows you to control and dictate your own body language so that you're sending the signals you want without giving up anything you'd prefer to keep to yourself.

Studies have concluded that in face-to-face communications, spoken words typically account for 7 percent of the received meaning. Tone of voice accounts for 38 percent, and body language is responsible for 55 percent. In short, the receiver is most likely to respond to either tone of voice or body language—not to the actual words used. Jury consultant Jo Ellen Dimitrius says that when jurors are asked what makes a witness appear confident, they cite body language twice as frequently as any other category. In other words, people "hear" with their eyes.

What is your body language saying about you? When you give a presentation or run a sales meeting, are you coming across as authoritative, confident, and credible or insecure, unreliable, and out of your league? Most importantly, how can you develop better language skills?

In fact, simply avoiding the most common mistakes and replacing them with more confident movements will make a big difference. Here are seven body language problems that will leave your audience unimpressed and alienated. Train yourself to avoid

them, and you'll see that simple changes can make all the difference. Here are a few things to be wary of.

Avoiding eye contact: This says you lack confidence and are nervous and unprepared. You should spend 90 percent or more of
any conversation looking into the eyes of your listeners. In formal
presentations, most people spend far too much time looking down
at notes, PowerPoint slides, or the table in front of them. Not
surprisingly, most speakers can change this behavior instantly
simply by watching a video of themselves. Powerful business
leaders look at their listeners directly in the eye when delivering
their message. Eye contact is by far the most important element
of body language. We'll have much more to say about it later in
this chapter.

Poor posture: Slouching says that you lack confidence and authority. When standing stationary, you should place your feet
at shoulder width and lean a bit forward. Pull your shoulders
slightly forward as well—you'll appear more energetic. Head and
spine should be straight. Don't use a tabletop or podium as an
excuse to lean on it.

Fidgeting or rigidity: Rocking back and forth or scratching
yourself makes you look nervous, unsure, or unprepared. So stop
fidgeting. On the other hand, don't stand there like a stone statue
either. Move around a bit, but make it appear there's a purpose.
Purposeful movement is not only acceptable in a conversation, it's
very welcome.

Unconvincing gestures: Gestures are fine; just don't overdo it.
Researchers have shown that gesturing reflects complex thought.
Gestures leave listeners with the perception of confidence, competence, and control. But the minute you try to copy a hand gesture, you risk looking contrived, like a bad politician. Don't use
gestures that seem incongruous with your words. The effect will
be like watching a video clip with mismatched audio.

The essential point is, you need to use your body as a communication tool fully equal to your words. Effective body language

will help you increase the energy of any contact, whether you're interviewing for a job, going on a first date, or negotiating an important purchase.

As mentioned above, eye contact is the most vital component of body language, so we're going to spend the rest of this chapter on that very misunderstood element.

Look into My Eyes

Eye contact is an aspect of nonverbal communication that is critical not only throughout human civilization but among many species of animals as well. The animal kingdom tends to perceive direct eye contact as a challenge or sign of aggression. For example, the Centers for Disease Control's dog bite prevention guide stresses the importance of avoiding eye contact with an unfamiliar dog. Dogs perceive direct eye contact as a sign of challenge and fight to maintain their position. Similar behavior has also been observed in bears and primates.

Maintaining eye contact during a conversation gives the impression that you are friendly and that you are paying attention to the other person. In some cultures, however, direct eye contact is considered rude or hostile. Understanding the message that you are sending through eye contact is important to improving communication in any environment.

It is important to understand the difference between eye contact and staring. While eye contact sends the message that you are confident, relaxed, and interested in what the other person has to say, staring is considered rude and even threatening. Understanding the difference between eye contact and staring is an advanced skill that can enhance your communication with others.

Staring involves looking solidly at the other person without a break. Many of us engaged in staring contests as children, and we still remember the uncomfortable feeling that generally accompanied the game. In a staring contest, the participants often avoid blinking, which leads to painful, watery eyes. Real-world staring does not necessarily mean failing to blink, but it does mean keeping one's eyes on another person without pausing. This behavior can make the other person feel uncomfortable, as if his or her personal space has been violated.

When maintaining normal eye contact, each person looks into the other's eyes and then away again. The speaker checks in visually with the listener, and the listener confirms understanding through meeting the speaker's eyes. This process cycles every few seconds throughout the duration of the conversation.

In the United States, avoiding eye contact sends the message that you are uncomfortable, perhaps because you have something to hide. You may be perceived as rude, unfriendly, or even arrogant. Depending on the circumstances, you may appear to be submissive or overdominant. Generally, a lack of eye contact when someone is speaking communicates submission, while avoiding eye contact when questioned indicates deceit.

The balance between too little eye contact and too much is delicate. Healthy eye contact within a two-way or small group conversation depends partly upon the group dynamics. If the conversational participants are familiar or emotionally close, a greater level of eye contact is often used. If the group members are naturally shy, however, less eye contact may occur. If you are in a new group and unsure how to use eye contact effectively, try mirroring the other participants.

Mirroring is a psychotherapeutic technique that is effective for communication with anyone. In mirroring, you actively pay attention to someone else's behavior and adjust yours to achieve similarity. Therefore, if the group seems to be looking back and forth from each other's eyes to the project at hand, try doing the same thing. In order to minimize confusion, you may wish to select just one person, perhaps the group leader, to mirror.

Public speaking situations require special care in eye contact. You will need to find a way to make each member of your audience feel drawn in, as if your speech is intended specifically for him or her.

In order to accomplish this, try sweeping the room with your eyes. Find one person in each section, seated near the middle of that section. Direct your gaze toward that person for four or five seconds, then move on to the next section and repeat the process. As you move back and forth between sections, be sure to pick out a new person each time. An older public speaking technique was to direct your gaze just over the heads of the audience, at a point on the back wall. However, this technique tends to lead to you locking your eyes on that spot, making those in the middle section feel that they are being stared at and those on the sides feel ignored.

Eye contact is an extremely important part of body language and nonverbal communication. In the United States and in many other countries, eye contact is crucial in job interviews, when asking someone for a date, and in many other important human interactions. If you are naturally shy, you may have difficulty maintaining eye contact. You can learn to improve your eye contact skills through practice, however. It may take a bit of work, but you will find the rewards of good eye contact to be well worth the effort.

ACTION STEPS

1. Think of a situation in which you were persuaded to do something or purchase something you were initially against. What persuaded you to change your mind?

2. Now think of something you need to persuade a coworker or friend to do and apply the techniques in this chapter to present your case and the benefits to that person. Record the outcome, what you learned as a result, and what you could do better next time.

ACTION PLAN NOTES

Today is life—the only life you are sure of. Make the most of today. Get interested in something. Shake yourself awake. Develop a hobby. Let the winds of enthusiasm sweep through you.

—Dale Carnegie

CHAPTER 10

Asking Questions Skillfully

Rules governing questions and answers are also undergoing continual revisions. What would have passed for a routine job interview twenty years ago might now be grounds for a federal lawsuit. Knowing how to ask questions is still a very important people skill, but now it's also a sensitive ethical and legal matter. In this chapter we'll begin to understand what has changed and what has not changed, and how you can make the most of the current realities.

GARBAGE IN, GARBAGE OUT

This well-known principle was originally linked to the operation of computer systems: If you put the wrong information in, you'll get the wrong information out. But the phrase has come to have a much wider application. No matter what kind of interpersonal exchange you're having, the information you receive will be dictated by the information you request. This is true of human communication in general. If you ask the wrong questions, you'll probably get the wrong answer. Or at least you won't get the answer you're hoping for.

The importance of this can't be overstated. Asking the right question is at the heart of effective communications and information exchange. But what exactly is the "right question" in a particular situation? You've got to answer that question in your own mind before you can ask anything of anyone else. To make matters worse, the right question today might not be the right question tomorrow, or even ten minutes from now. Questioning, therefore, is a very sophisticated people skill, whether it takes place in a job interview or in a conversation with your teenage son or daughter.

By learning to ask the right questions in a particular situation, you can improve a whole range of communications skills. At the very least, you can avoid offending people—which is the most frequent result of ill-advised questioning. But that's only the beginning. Skillful questioning will allow you to gather better information and learn more about the people in your life. You can build stronger relationships, manage your responsibilities more effectively, and help others to do the same.

Here are some common questioning techniques—and when (and when not) to use them.

OPEN AND CLOSED QUESTIONS

A closed question is one that calls for a one-word word or very brief answer. "Are you thirsty?" The answer is either yes or no. "Where do you live?" Depending on the circumstances, the answer may be the name of your hometown or your street address.

Open questions elicit longer answers. They usually include "what," "why," or "how." An open question asks for information, an opinion, or feelings. Often they begin with a wide-angle invitation such as "Tell me" or "Describe for me."

Some other examples include: "What happened at the

meeting?" "Why did you react that way?" "How was your vacation?" "Tell me what happened next." "Describe the accident in more detail."

Open questions are good for developing an extended conversation, getting more detail about a specific situation, and exploring someone's opinions and feelings. Closed questions provide factual understanding or bring closure to an otherwise unresolved factual matter. But both kinds of questions, if they're asked at the wrong time or in the wrong way, can do more harm than good in an interpersonal exchange.

FUNNEL QUESTIONS

As a way of utilizing the best of both forms of questions, it can be useful to begin with open questions and then gradually shift to inquiries that are more sharply focused. Imagine, for example, that a police officer is interviewing witnesses to an altercation in the street. The dialogue might go something like this:

"How many people were involved in the fight?"

"About ten."

"Were they kids or adults?"

"Mostly kids."

"What ages were they?"

"About fourteen or fifteen."

"Were any of them wearing anything distinctive?"

"Yes, some of them had red baseball caps."

"Can you remember if there was a logo on any of the caps?"

"Actually, I remember seeing a big letter Z."

Using this technique, the officer helps the witness review the event and gradually identify useful details. It's unlikely the officer would have gotten this information if he'd simply asked an open question at the start, such as "Are there any details you can give me about what you saw?"

This technique is known as funnel questioning. It starts with closed questions. As the parties progress through the funnel, the questions become more and more narrow.

Funnel questions are good for finding out more detail about a specific incident. The technique also builds confidence and trust on the part of the person who's being asked the questions.

PROBING QUESTIONS

Here are some other strategies for finding out more detail. Sometimes it's as simple as asking for an example about a previous statement. Or you can solicit additional information for the sake of clarity: "When do you need this report, and do you want to see a draft before I give you my final version?"; "How do you know that the new database can't be used by the sales force?"

Generally speaking, probing questions are good for gaining clarification and understanding of previously rendered facts, and also for drawing information out of people who are trying to avoid telling you something.

There's a refinement of the probing questions technique known as the Five Whys method, which was created in the 1970s for internal use by the Toyota Corporation. The system is based on the fact that a "why?" question usually generates another, more sharply focused "why?" The system begins by looking at the end result and then works backward toward the root cause by continually asking why? For example:

- Why is our client unhappy? Because we did not deliver our services when we said we would.

- Why were we unable to meet the delivery schedule? Because the job took much longer than we thought it would.

- Why did it take so much longer? Because we underestimated the complexity of the work.

- Why did we underestimate the complexity of the work? Because we made a quick estimate of the time needed to complete the project and did not list the individual stages needed to complete it.

- Why did we rely on only a quick estimate? Because we were running behind on other projects. We need to evaluate our time scheduling and specification procedures.

Because the Five Whys strategy is so simple, it can be adapted quickly and applied to most any problem.

LEADING QUESTIONS

This kind of question is intended to lead people to your way of thinking. This can happen in several ways.

With an assumption: "How late do you think the project will be?" This assumes that the project will certainly not be completed on time.

By adding a personal appeal to agree at the end: "She's very efficient, don't you think?" or "It will be better to wait another week, don't you think?"

By phrasing the question so that the reflexive response is yes: In this way, "Shall we all approve the bid?" is more likely to get a positive response than "Do you want to approve the bid or not?" A further refinement is to make the question personal: "Would you like me to go ahead and approve the bid?" rather than just "Shall I approve it?"

Leading questions tend to be closed-ended. They're best for getting the answer you want while still leaving the other person feeling that they had a choice. The danger of leading questions is that they can seem manipulative or even dishonest. In the past, they've often been abused by high-pressure salesmen or even con artists. If you become aware that you're being asked lots of leading questions, keep your guard up—or ask some leading questions of your own.

RHETORICAL QUESTIONS

These aren't really questions at all, because they don't expect an answer. They're really just statements phrased in question form: "Isn't it a beautiful day?"; "Don't you just love Christmas?"

Rhetorical questions are a way of engaging a listener. As a people skill, these questions are a good way of eliciting an almost automatic agreement. Once that agreement has been obtained, a questioner will sometimes use the momentum in order to gain a more substantial concession. For instance, a string of rhetorical questions can lead to one that isn't rhetorical at all. "Isn't that a great paint job on this new car?" "Don't you love the way the color seems to shimmer in the light?" "Wouldn't you love to have a car that looked like that for your very own?"

USING QUESTIONING TECHNIQUES

At one time or another, you have probably used all of these questioning techniques, whether at work or at home. But by consciously applying the appropriate kind of questioning, you can gain the information, response, or outcome that you want even more effectively. What could be more of a people skill than that?

QUESTIONS ARE A POWERFUL WAY OF:

Learning: Ask open and closed questions, and use probing questioning.

Relationship building: People generally respond positively if you ask about what they do or inquire about their opinions. If you do this in an affirmative way—"Tell me what you like best about working here"—you will help to build and maintain an open dialogue.

Managing: Rhetorical and leading questions are useful here too. They can help get people to reflect and to commit to courses of action that you've suggested: "Wouldn't it be great to gain some further qualifications?"

Avoiding misunderstandings: Use probing questions to seek clarification, particularly when the consequences are significant. Make sure you avoid jumping to conclusions.

Calming conflict: You can calm an angry customer or colleague by using funnel questions to get them to go into more detail about their grievance. This will not only distract them from their emotions but will often help you to identify a small practical thing that you can do. It is often enough to make them feel that they have "won" something and no longer need to be angry.

Persuading people: No one likes to be lectured, but asking a series of open questions will help others to embrace the reasons behind your point of view. "What do you think about bringing the sales force in for half a day to have their laptops upgraded?"

Skillful *questioning* needs to be matched by careful *listening* so that you understand what people really mean with their answers. Make sure that you give the person you're questioning enough time to respond. They may need to include thinking time before they answer, so don't just interpret a pause as a "No comment." Patience is a people skill!

ACTION STEPS

1. Think about a person with whom you would like to build a better relationship. Record five questions you can ask them in order to establish rapport and learn more about their interests and values.

2. If you are going to be interviewing for a job in the near future, prepare five specific questions targeting that company or industry that would help you determine if this position is a good fit for you.

ACTION PLAN NOTES

Talk is a voyage with a purpose, and the purpose must be charted. A person who starts out going nowhere usually gets there.

—Dale Carnegie

CHAPTER 11

Assertive Speaking

It is no secret that the ability to communicate well is an essential people skill. That's always been true. But what's involved in good communication is always changing, especially in corporate settings. Years ago, for example, there were far fewer women in the business world than there are today. Communication was largely a male-to-male experience. Now, however, in a much more diverse workplace, there are many new issues to be aware of in all forms of business communication. What's more, constantly evolving new technologies such as email, voice mail, text messaging, and cell phones have created new categories of communication. These technologies have hugely increased the pace and efficiency of business contact, but they've also expanded the possibilities for mistakes and misunderstandings. We'll be looking at these changes and many other related topics in this chapter and in the one that follows.

In this chapter our discussion will focus on the third essential people skill, assertive communication—specifically, speaking. We will share principles and applications that address one-on-one encounters as well as meetings and presentations. In chapter 12, we'll concentrate on assertive listening. Listening is definitely one of the most undervalued people skills, and it deserves a chapter of its own.

In any field of endeavor, there's an important difference between participation and competence. Someone may be able to speak the English language, but this doesn't mean that he can be effective as a professional speaker. Another person may be capable of writing complete sentences, but that alone won't enable her to get a book published. With this distinction in mind, the first step toward effective, assertive communication is understanding that this really is a skill. Just talking is not communication, nor is just writing. These are areas that require attention, practice, and continuous improvement. They take work, especially when you're just starting to realize the importance of good communication to your success in a management role. It may surprise you to realize that even seemingly casual conversations should be handled carefully in a corporate setting. So often, something is said in an informal context, and only later does it become clear that this was the cause of a misunderstanding.

EFFECTIVE COMMUNICATION TAKES SOME PLANNING

In general, most business conversations are not planned; they more or less drift along. As a leader, you need to strike a balance between friendly communication and efficient, assertive sharing of information. If you're planning on a more formal conversation for a significant purpose, you'll first need to clearly identify that purpose in your own mind. Then you'll need a plan for achieving it in a face-to-face encounter. True, some people are good at "thinking on their feet," but this is generally because they already have a clear understanding of the context and their own goals. Most of us need to plan, however, and as you do so, here are three key points to bear in mind.

First, you need to make sure that your message is understood.

Second, you must understand what is being said to you, even if the speaker is not an especially good communicator. We'll have much more to say about this element when we discuss the topic of assertive listening.

Third, you need to maintain control of the conversation. Make sure the necessary points are addressed, and pertinent questions are effectively addressed. Needless to say, all this should take place within a reasonable time frame.

THE DYNAMICS OF COMMUNICATION

In order to understand how these points can be satisfied, we need to look at what actually takes place when people talk with one another. It's much more of a creative process than you might have realized. The process includes not only understanding what is actually being said but also grasping the speaker's motives, his implicit but unspoken messages, and any irony or sarcasm that could run completely counter to the explicit meaning of the words. In short, there's a lot going on when people try to communicate. By using easy-to-follow, unambiguous language and a clear tone of voice, you can make it easier for others to understand exactly what you're thinking, feeling, and wanting. This is equally valuable whether you're trying to solve a problem with a team member or expressing appreciation or concern.

Carefully planning how you express yourself might appear to take a great deal of time, but in the long run it's worthwhile. This is true especially when you factor in the time required to unscramble misunderstandings and to work through the feelings that usually accompany not being understood. When you do this, you'll see that expressing yourself more carefully can actually save you time and perhaps save money for your company as well.

If you observe people in conversation, you'll begin to notice that human communication typically leaves many things unsaid.

It depends on the listener to fill in the missing-but-implied information. For example, an assistant may say to an executive, "Your two o'clock is here." If we rely only on what's being directly said, this statement makes no sense at all. Of course, the assistant means, "Your client who made an appointment for two o'clock has arrived in the waiting room." Of course, the executive understands the abbreviated message, and most of the time, this process works very well. In situations of change, ambiguity, conflict, or intense deadline pressure, however, the "shorthand" way of speaking may not work at all. There are several reasons for this.

For instance, your listeners may fill in a completely different set of details than the one you intended, or they may not understand the significance of what you are saying. They may get only some of the details and miss the big picture. Perhaps without actually intending to mislead anyone, you may leave out important elements because of the reactions you think they will elicit. Since misunderstanding can be very costly both personally and professionally, you need both to help your listeners by giving them a complete picture in language that doesn't confuse or mislead them.

THE FIVE CONVERSATION TOOLS

Research has shown that there are five main tools that your conversation partners can use to re-create your experience inside their minds. The more elements you provide for them, the higher the probability that your listener's re-creation will match the message you wish to convey. Let's look at the tools one by one.

TOOL 1: *Stick to the Facts*

First, what have you seen, heard, or otherwise experienced that you want to convey to your listener? Here it's important to stick to just the facts. What happened, or what didn't happen? When did it happen, or when was it supposed to happen? For example: "I got your memo this morning about the new client in Florida." Or, "I haven't yet received the report on the latest customer survey. I think we agreed that was due last Thursday."

TOOL 2: *Share the Feelings That the Facts Elicit Within You*

Second, what feelings do the facts bring out in you? Obviously, in a business setting, you'll be dealing with a relatively narrow range of emotions. You might be pleased about something that's happened, excited about something that's going to happen, or disappointed about something that you thought would happen but didn't. An example might be "I'm really happy that you handled the situation so smoothly" or "When a shipment gets lost like this, I begin to lose confidence in the way we fill our orders."

TOOL 3: *Share What You Are Experiencing*

Third, what interpretations, wants, needs, memories, or anticipations of yours support those feelings? Once again, a business conversation is different from delivering a toast at your daughter's wedding. There's no need to become emotional, but you can and should share some of what you experience as a leader dealing with many different people and projects. If your company is having problems with a new voice-mail system, for example, you might mention that the savings that result from an automated system might not really be cost-efficient. If potential clients become frustrated with talking to a machine and hang up, at could be a good argument for having a live phone receptionist. You might mention the fact that more business is lost because of an unsatisfactory phone experience than for any other reason.

TOOL 4: *Define What You Want*

What action, information, or commitment do you want now? This is really the key segment of the conversation. This is what you've been leading up to, and this is where you want to be an assertive communicator in the best possible sense. It's best if you introduce what you're going to say in a more or less formal manner, which will make clear to the listener that this is the time to pay attention. The best way to do this is with a very simple phrase: "May I make a suggestion?" There's simply no better way to say it. In fact, if you always say "May I make a suggestion?" it will almost become a conditioned reflex for team members to perk up their ears. Then you're in a position to give a directive in a very positive context, because you've asked permission to do so.

TOOL 5: *Include a Benefit-Oriented Conclusion*

Finally, always include a benefit-oriented conclusion with any suggestion you might make. A typical sequence could go something like this: "I'm glad to hear you were able to close that sale over the phone. It's really much more efficient to do that than to have a face-to-face meeting. May I make a suggestion? When it looks like the client wants a live sales call, ask if you can handle it over the phone, provided of course that your relationship with the client is already well established. If you can do that, your commissions are bound to go up, because you'll be making more sales in a shorter period of time."

This five-part template is a hugely powerful tool for effectively assertive business conversations. It's so simple and logical, yet very few people are able to discover it on their own. Many times, managers lead off with point number two (the feelings that are being aroused in them), and can often do so in a very inappropriate manner. This is especially true when the feelings are negative. "I get really angry when something like this happens!"

In one form or another, this phrase is spoken literally thousands of times every day in companies across the country. But what does it really convey? The emphasis is on what the manager is feeling, while true masters of leadership emphasize the business issue at hand.

These five assertive conversation tools can be very effective, but they're not all that is required in effective of one-on-one business communication. It's always a good idea to ask for confirmation that what you've said has been clearly understood. It's also a good idea to ask in a diplomatic way for any reservations or objections. The truth is, those objections are almost always present, but they won't surface unless you ask for them.

QUESTIONS ARE A GOOD SIGN

When speaking, you can make an effort to deal with any objections in advance by adding information that will make your message better understood. By the same token, when others are speaking, you should deliberately ask questions to establish the context of their thinking. If there are no questions on the part of either you or your listeners, there's a good chance that the communication will be less than ideal.

This is a really important point. As managers move up the corporate ladder to senior executive positions, it's easy for them to believe that everyone admires and agrees with them. Ideally, this is in fact the case, but it may also be that team members are simply afraid to speak their minds. As a leader, you should assume that people have something to question or add to what you've told them. If those opinions are not made available to you, you should likewise assume that you have not successfully completed the conversation. In this sense, an assertive business talk is like a sales call. Unless the customers' objections are brought to the surface, buyer's remorse will almost always set in and there may be negative repercussions later. So don't let your ego convince you that everything has been understood and accepted. In fact, you should operate on the opposite assumption.

Once you've heard the objections to your message, you should use a basic technique of interpersonal dynamics. That is, you should repeat and confirm what you've just heard. Once again, there's a very simple way to move toward this in one sentence. Just say, "Let me be sure I understand what you're saying." Then repeat what you've just been told, not word for word, but in a slightly different form. Rephrase what your team member has communicated in a way that shows you've heard it, understood it, and thoughtfully evaluated it. Keep in mind also that it's not always necessary to deal with objections at the very moment that you first hear them. Give yourself some time to respond in the best possible way. The first thing you need to do is to bring the objections to the surface. The second is to show that you understand them and take them seriously. State your message, ask questions that bring out objections, and then make sure that you understand and respect them.

WRITE AND SHARE SIGNIFICANT IDEAS

If, in your judgment, a conversation has dealt with substantial issues, take the time to make a written record of what transpired and email it to the appropriate parties. Surprisingly, this is almost more important for encounters that take place at the water cooler than for full-blown meetings in a conference room. Sometimes very important decisions are made spontaneously and with little fanfare. New ideas can be introduced. Seeds can be planted that, if handled correctly, can develop into important projects.

Writing an email message in this context is one of the best uses of the new information technologies. It's a way of quickly creating and circulating a reminder. While it may not become tremendously significant, there's always a chance that it might. There are other benefits as well. Your email can provide or ask for further clarification. In other words, is this what we discussed and agreed upon? And in writing down your thoughts, you may recognize questions or omissions that were overlooked in the initial conversation.

DEALING WITH CONFLICT CONSTRUCTIVELY

Even if you use all the tools and techniques we've been discussing, there are still times when conversations will turn into confrontation and conflict. Let's face this reality very directly by looking once again at what assertiveness really means. To assert, according to one dictionary, means "to declare or to state clearly." This should always be your aim. Assertiveness doesn't mean winning. It doesn't mean scoring more conversational points. If people argue with you or even lose their tempers, just remain calmly assertive. As you do so, here's a two-part template you can use for guidance:

First, acknowledge what is being said by showing an understanding of the other party's position, or simply rephrasing it, as we discussed earlier. In the context of a heated discussion, this is a polite way of saying "I heard you already."

Then state your own point of view clearly and concisely, with a little supporting evidence. Be careful not to provide too much supporting evidence, however, as you don't want to come across as if you were building a case in a court of law. Now state clearly what you would like to happen next. This is a way of moving the discussion forward rather than continuing to fight it out on the same ground.

No doubt there will be times when a very forceful argument on your part will bring about a positive outcome. But there will also be times when this will get you nowhere, particularly with people who don't want to listen. Sometimes these individuals will be subordinates, but often you'll find yourself stonewalled by senior management. If that's the case, you should agree with the decision of the senior manager, but you should also make your objections and your reasons clearly known. If you think you're in the right, say so. Allow your team members the same freedom. Always be open to the possibility that someone who disagrees with you might be correct. If events prove this to be the case, then acknowledge that fact gracefully.

If and when you have a difficult encounter, be professional. Don't lose your self-control, even if you want to make it appear that you've done exactly that. If you deliberately seem to lose your temper for effect, make that a conscious decision. Remember that insults are fundamentally ineffective. Calling people names is just distracting. They are unlikely to listen to what you have to say. In the short term you may feel some satisfaction or excitement, but this comes with the price of a prolonged and intensified argument.

As a corollary, it must be emphasized that profanity should not be a part of assertive communication. This is less an issue of morality than of simple human nature. If certain words are included in a conversation, particularly with an angry tone, those become the hot words, the only words that the listener really hears. In this sense, profanity actually undermines the content of your message and, of course, to many people it's truly distasteful or even offensive. Instead of reacting immediately and saying something you might regret, take a step back and postpone your reaction.

COMMUNICATION IN MEETINGS AND PRESENTATIONS

So far we've focused on spoken communications between one person and another. For the balance of this chapter, we'll look at group communications of the kind that occur in meetings and presentations.

In any company, meetings are a vital part to the assignment of work and the flow of information. Meetings are the vehicles for gathering resources from many sources and directing them toward a common goal. However, meetings are widely disliked. Most people feel they are usually futile, boring, time wasting, dull, and inconvenient.

As a leader, your challenge is to break this perception and to make your meetings effective. As with every other significant form of communication, meetings should be planned ahead of time, carefully directed while they are in progress, and reviewed afterward for what went well and what could be improved upon. Really, a meeting is the ultimate form of managed conversation within a business setting. If you can gain a reputation for holding decisive, effective meetings, your team members will value this efficiency and will prepare well so that their contribution will be heard. At the same time, your supervisors will take notice of your work in this difficult area.

Attendees

For any meeting, the first question is always, Who should attend? Be strict! A meeting loses its effectiveness if too many people are involved. If someone insists on attending, explain that it's not really necessary and politely but firmly dissuade them. Usually, most people are only too happy to be released from another meeting.

Duration

How long should you plan for the meeting to last? It may seem difficult to predict the length of a meeting, but you must try to do so. Conversations tend to fill the available time, so if the meeting is open-ended, it will drift on forever. You should designate a time for the end of the meeting so that everyone can plan the rest of the day with confidence.

Make the time limit for the meeting known in advance to

everyone who will attend, and remind the attendees at the beginning of the meeting. Often there's a tendency to view meetings as a time of relaxation, since no one person has to be active throughout. You can change this view by emphasizing the time limit: "This is what we have to accomplish, and this is how long we have to get it done." If an important new topic arises unexpectedly during the discussion, stay with the planned agenda. The new topic should then be dealt with at a separate meeting.

Agenda

The purpose of a meeting agenda is to inform participants of the subject of the meeting in advance and to structure the discussion of the meeting itself. To inform people beforehand and to solicit ideas, circulate a draft agenda and ask for comments. Then create a revised agenda and get it back to the participants as soon as possible.

The final agenda states the purpose of each section of the meeting. There should be an objective for each section. If that objective can't be summarized in a few points, it is probably too complex. The purpose of the meeting should be sufficiently precise that it can be summarized in a brief heading at the top of the printed agenda.

Coordinating Contributions

While the meeting is in progress, as the leader and facilitator you must assertively coordinate the contributions of everyone present. The degree of control that you exercise over the meeting can vary throughout. If you start things off on the right foot, a meeting can run itself, especially if the participants know each other well. You must always be ready, however, to step in to complete the meeting objectives.

Purpose

The purpose of a meeting may suggest a specific way to conduct the event. For example, if the purpose is to share information, the meeting might begin with a formal presentation followed by questions. If the purpose is to seek information on how to deal with a specific issue, it might start with a short statement of the problem and then progress to an open discussion or brainstorming session. If the goal of the meeting is to arrive at a decision of some kind, the group might review the options, establish the criteria to be applied, agree on how the decision should be made, and then proceed to make it. Bear in mind that the success of a meeting often depends on the confidence level of the participants. All pertinent ideas should be welcome. No one should be laughed at or dismissed, and even weak ideas should be treated seriously. All these guidelines should be diligently followed in the spirit of assertive communication and good people skills.

In closing this discussion of spoken communication and people skills, it's interesting to note just how basic this issue is to human success. The biblical story of the Tower of Babel is a good illustration. It depicts a civilization's attempt to construct an edifice so tall that it could actually reach the heavens. The Bible tells us that the project was a success. The tower was getting higher and higher with no sign of slowing down. This, of course, was not the way that mankind was ordained to enter Paradise, so the Creator brought the project to an end. That did not require bolts of lightning or an earthquake, however. The Creator simply introduced the idea of language into the world. People could no longer understand what they were saying to one another, and progress on the Tower of Babel came to a halt.

While you may not think of your company as a medium for getting to heaven, it is a collective enterprise that depends completely on good communication. If you and your team members can't share ideas in a proactive and supportive manner, nothing else really matters. Failure to communicate spells doom for any shared enterprise. On the other hand, literally anything is possible when people are able to work together. Keep this in mind whenever you speak with your team members, and you can accomplish more than you ever imagined.

ACTION STEPS

1. We often assume that we are communicating effectively and that our directives are understood. This is not always the case, however. For the next week, check your communication skills by verifying, with those to whom you have communicated, that the message received was the message you intended to deliver. You can do this by simply asking them to repeat what you just said for clarification purposes.

2. When communicating, ideally you should incorporate the following five tools to your presentation repertoire:

   Tool 1: Stick to the facts

   Tool 2: Share the feelings that the facts elicit within you

   Tool 3: Share what you are experiencing

   Tool 4: Define what you want

   Tool 5: Include a benefit-oriented conclusion

Take some time to write out a presentation, ideally one that you can use at an upcoming meeting. Then go through the five tools above to ensure that you have applied all five to your speech.

Then make note of any new findings that you discover in response to the presentation and its effectiveness.

3. Dealing with conflict constructively in the workplace can be difficult. Which of the following areas could you work on to further develop your conflict resolution skills? Place an X or check beside those areas that you feel require some additional attention, then devise a plan to develop those skills and integrate them into your daily routine.

☐ I declare or state clearly my intention.

☐ My agenda is not to win but to score more conversation points.

☐ I remain calmly assertive.

☐ I acknowledge what is being said by showing an understanding of the other party's position.

☐ I state my own point of view clearly and concisely, with a little supporting evidence.

☐ I state clearly what I would like to happen next.

☐ When necessary, I agree to the decision of senior management.

☐ When necessary, I make my objections and my reasons clearly known.

☐ I am open to the possibility that someone who disagrees with me might be correct.

☐   I remain cool and do not lose my self-control.

☐   I do not insult or call people names.

☐   If I have a difficult encounter, I always behave professionally.

ACTION PLAN NOTES

This is one of the most basic facts of human psychology.
We are flattered by other people's attention. It makes us feel
special. We want to be around people who show interest in
us. We want to keep them close. And we tend to reciprocate
their interest by showing interest in them.

—Dale Carnegie

CHAPTER 12

Assertive Listening

Listening is an art, a skill, and a discipline, and like other skills, it needs self-control. As a leader, you must understand what is involved in listening and develop the necessary techniques to be silent and pay attention to what you're hearing. You must learn to ignore your own needs and concentrate attention on the person speaking. Hearing becomes listening only when you pay attention to what is being said and follow it very closely.

Without question, listening is an absolutely essential people skill. Research shows that most people spend 70 percent of their waking hours interacting with other human beings in some way, shape, or form, and 45 percent of that time is spent listening. As with any activity to which you devote a large part of your day, it's better to be good at it than poor. Assertive listening is being good at listening, and the first step in this direction is to understand what really goes on during a human conversational interaction.

OBEYING THE CONVERSATION RULES

Analogies are never perfect, but there is an analogy that comes extremely close to precisely and exactly explaining what goes on when people speak and listen. It's an analogy between human communication and driving your car in traffic. Almost certainly, you've never met most of the people who are in their cars all around you, but when your cars arrive at a stop sign together, it's understood that everyone will stop. By the rules of the road, the car on the right has the right-of-way, and most people respect this. They let the car on the right proceed into the intersection first. Sometimes people even give a little wave to urge the other driver forward, and usually the other driver will give a little wave of thanks in return. This is just how it works, and after people have been driving for a while, they understand the various protocols and abide by them.

Of course, there are exceptions. Some people speed. Others drive too slowly. At stop signs, some people don't yield the right-of-way, and others may blow through the intersection without even stopping. This is extremely irresponsible and dangerous behavior, and there are penalties attached to it. There are traffic tickets and license suspensions, not to mention the possibility of a life-threatening accident.

A conversation works in basically the same way, although the stop signs and traffic signals are a little subtler. You may not know the person you're speaking with, but experience has taught you that there are moments when it's your turn to listen and times when it's your turn to speak. There are no physical stop signs to indicate these places, but you've learned to sense them and respect them. Just as certain intersections can be complex and congested, conversations involving several people can require greater awareness on everyone's part. Even if there are four or five people talking, things can go smoothly if all parties obey the rules.

Once again, however, there is the problem of people who don't obey the rules. There are conversational speeders, whose verbal rpm are always in overdrive. There are people who talk so slowly and softly that listening to them is like being stuck behind an old farmer in a pickup truck on a two-lane country road. Then there are the really dangerous conversationalists, who seem determined to cause accidents through rudeness and insensitivity. The unfortunate thing about these rule breakers is that there are no traffic cops to get them off the road, and they take full advantage of that fact. Since there's no law enforcement mechanism for verbal traffic patterns, they indulge themselves to the fullest.

When you're driving your car, chances are you'd like to drive as fast as safely possible in order to get to your destination in the shortest time. You don't actually drive that fast, but maybe you do go five or ten miles an hour above the speed limit on the interstate. What about when you're engaged in a conversation? Do you go 60 in the 55 zone? Do you come to a complete halt at the stop signs, or do you just slow down and glide through?

Just as you may drive a bit above the speed limit, there's also a high probability that you're more focused on talking than listening. To become an assertive listener, you first need to become aware of that tendency, and then you need to change it.

EMPATHETIC LISTENING

We all want to speak, and we all want to be listened to. Do you know what it means, though, to listen, to really listen? It is more than just hearing the words. It is truly understanding other people's messages as well as their circumstances and feelings. This is the meaning of empathy, and empathy is a basic element of assertive listening. Empathy means understanding other people so well that, at least for the moment, you experience their feelings. It's listening so intently and identifying so closely that you experience the other person's situation, thoughts, and emotions. Good friends do this; so do good doctors, and so do good leaders.

Assertive, empathetic listening shows that you care and understand other people. When they sense this on your part, they'll naturally feel more comfortable and confident in their communication with you. They will trust you and open up more. If they feel you've misunderstood them, they'll sense that it's okay to correct your impression. As a result, you'll get a clearer and more accurate sense of what's really being said.

In short, assertive listening lets you learn more about your team members. It cuts through the superficiality of conversation and brings out what's really on people's minds. As an assertive listener, you're able to direct the conversation toward important topics without ever needing to do so in a formal way. Since the speaker knows it's safe to talk about these subjects, he or she can express real feelings. This is not just good business practice on your part, it is genuinely caring behavior.

At first, assertive listening may require some focused attention and effort, but you'll quickly see that it actually makes business conversations easier. It can reduce the impatience that is so often a part of business interactions. It can also eliminate mistaken negative assumptions, since you will have developed a greater understanding of what the other person engaged in the conversation is really like. Assertive listening is one of the more important people skills you will ever acquire. It's amazing how few people do it well.

CONVERSATIONAL BARRIERS TO AVOID

Assertive listening, as we've discussed, is based on truly wanting to know the other person. It also depends on avoiding some very common conversational barriers. Let's look at a few of these right now.

First, avoid constantly comparing yourself to the speaker. Most people don't come right out and say it, but when someone else is talking, their minds are filled with thoughts like "Am I smarter than this person?" "Have I had a rougher life than this person?" or, especially, "I can't wait for this guy to stop talking so that I can tell an anecdote of my own—which, by the way, is much more interesting than what I'm now hearing."

This last tendency is very significant. Once you become aware of it, you'll be amazed how often it turns up both in your own thoughts and in conversations you take part in. Zig Ziglar calls it "playing topper." It's the impulse to immediately top the other person's story. Someone says, "My plane was delayed in Chicago for two hours," and you immediately flash, "I was delayed in Denver for three hours." He says, "I broke my arm," and you think, "I broke my leg." She tells you, "I caught a big fish," and you're instantly scanning your memory for the biggest fish you ever caught, or maybe the biggest fish your brother-in-law caught, provided it was a really big one. That's what playing topper is all about. It's so common you'll recognize it right away, and no doubt you can see why it's the deadly enemy of assertive listening.

AVOID MIND READING

A second barrier involves trying to read the mind of the person talking, as opposed to listening to what he's saying. If someone says, "I really like working here," you interpret this to mean "He doesn't like working here, but he says that he does because he's afraid of losing his job." This is mind reading, not listening. Once again, it's concentrating on your own powers of interpretation instead of hearing what people are saying and, for the moment at least, giving them the benefit of the doubt.

The third obstacle to listening assertively is called filtering. Basically, it means perking up your ears when you hear something that interests you or that you agree with and shutting down your attention to the rest. A big part of all conversation, whether business or personal, is about establishing a sense of complicity or shared interest with the other person. If that sense of shared interest or agreement isn't forthcoming, there's a tendency to discount what someone is saying. Furthermore, if the speaker indicates an interest in something you're absolutely not interested in at all, you may even decide to tune that person out completely. If someone tells you that he attends NASCAR events every weekend and owns a pit bull, you may devalue his ideas for your business simply because you're not a fan of NASCAR and you prefer cats over dogs. This person may have some excellent ideas on marketing strategy, but you'll never know.

Beyond these three barriers, there are many, many more. Lots of people are judgmental: They decide a statement is "crazy," "boring," "immature," or "hostile," even before it's completed. Other people have a therapeutic approach to conversation, silently drafting their prescriptions and advice throughout the dialogue. Perhaps you experience every conversation as an intellectual debate, with the goal of defeating the opponent. Maybe you are convinced that you're always right about business issues, so what's the point of listening? If you're afraid of having a serious conversation, you might keep making jokes in order to keep things light. For that same reason, you might just keep agreeing with the person in order to remain safely in your comfort zone.

As you read these obstacles to assertive listening, there's an excellent chance that you saw yourself in at least some of them. That's good. There's no way to change a behavior until you first know that it exists.

Due to these and other barriers that are inherent in most conversations, people typically recall only 65 percent of what they hear twenty minutes after a discussion has taken place. Assertive listening isn't easy. It's not even natural, given that the obstacles we've just looked at are natural expressions of interpersonal psychology. Our concentration lasts only a short time before we get distracted. This happens to everyone, but assertive listeners make an effort to get back on track. They ask clarifying questions, and they reassure the speaker that the message is being heard and understood. Above all, assertive listeners guard against prejudices and biases, closed-minded opinions, and inner defenses that prevent us from hearing what is really being said. To keep this from happening, remember something that Mark Twain once wrote: "If we were supposed to talk more than we listen, we'd have two mouths and one ear."

POOR LISTENING RESPONSES

As you listen, you must also respond. Why? So that you can listen some more! Of course, even poor listeners respond in one way or another, but there's a wide spectrum of responses that extends from outright hostility all the way to true empathy. Right now, let's take a quick look at that spectrum from bottom to top, from callous indifference to genuinely assertive listening.

At the bottom of the listening scale, we find people who not only wish the topic would change but also who come right out and change it. Someone says, "I think we should have fewer meetings on Fridays," and the listener says, "How about those Mets?"

One step up from this is the "I know better." The speaker says, "My computer crashed," and you say, "I doubt that. I'll take a look at it when I have time." Often the listener will add (or at least think) something further, such as "You should have read the instruction manual" or, "I can see that you're technologically challenged."

An extension of this is the judgmental response. To a person who says he ate too much at lunch, you respond, "Obesity is a national disgrace, and it's driving up the cost of health insurance." This is an extreme example, of course, but the impulse to judge is very strong in many of us. Assertive listening demands that we take off our judicial robes, at least for the duration of the conversation.

Next comes the advising response, which is a less moralistic form of judgment.

A colleague of yours tells you he is afraid about asking for a raise. Instead of responding to what he wants you to hear (that he is afraid), you tell him what to write in a memo to the boss. Or, along the same lines, you could devalue what he's feeling under the guise of reassurance. You might say something like, "Oh, everybody gets nervous about asking for more money. Just don't let it get to you." In other words, I don't want to hear any more about it.

Once again, most of us are guilty of some of these unempathetic responses. If it happened on only a few occasions there would be no problem, but poor listening skills seem to be habit-forming. We become habitual topic changers or advisers. Of course, the best way to end a bad habit is not to suppress it but to replace it with a good habit. Let's look at how to move up the scale of listening responses toward the positive and assertive options.

POSITIVE ASSERTIVE LISTENING OPTIONS

The first of these options is to correct any assumed understanding of some of the other person's thoughts, feelings, or circumstances. You may hear some of what's being said or implied but not all of it. In turn you formulate some conclusions in your head. If the speaker picks up on this, it may discourage him or her from saying anything further. Since this limited understanding is often an unconscious process on the part of the listener, it's important to train yourself to ask for clarification and elaboration, even if you don't think it's really necessary. Don't assume that you've heard everything you need to know. In fact, assume the opposite.

Above this response level we begin to approach really assertive listening. Now you respond with genuine empathy. You really put yourself in another person's shoes. Your comments reflect what the speaker has told you. As you listen, your comments are brief and accurate. You paraphrase and mirror what you've heard, but you do so in your own words and in a way that seems respectful and natural. As a result, the speaker knows you are listening closely and that you care about what he has said. What we say is a reflection on our listening skills.

All this takes some real skill and technique. It's best, for example, to phrase your comments somewhat tentatively, because empathy questions are actually statements. When you ask, "Are you feeling down?" you're really saying, "I can see that you're sad about something." Even when you're slightly off the mark, a tentative approach gives the speaker a chance to set the record straight and get you precisely in tune. For this reason, it's important to make frequent comments that reflect your understanding of what's just been said. If the speaker gets no comment from you for two or three minutes, he or she may conclude that you've lost interest or disapprove of what you're hearing or don't understand it.

PROVIDING CONSTRUCTIVE FEEDBACK

As you become more experienced and adept with assertive listening, you'll reach a totally new level of response. Here something really amazing will happen: You'll often be able to understand what people are thinking and feeling sometimes before they themselves know it. In fact, you can help them to gain that level of insight through the questions you ask. More often than not, they'll appreciate your feedback and will embrace your interpretation and analysis. As an assertive listener, you'll know exactly when to present your ideas in this way. It's not something you'll want to do too soon. If you give an interpretation too quickly, it may seem too personal, critical, or premature. So once again, it's wise to be tentative. Phrases like "I'm wondering if . . ." or "It sounds to me like . . ." can be very useful.

Genuinely assertive listeners can often share insights that are not only useful but positively life transforming. Dale Carnegie was certainly such a listener, and the tools and techniques he mastered have been brought to the world through his books and training programs. You may wonder whether you can ever achieve that level of people skills. Don't worry, though. Nothing that Dale Carnegie accomplished is out of your reach, and that's especially true in the area of listening and assertive communication.

ADDITIONAL LISTENING TECHNIQUES

To complete this chapter, let's sum up some of the central points of this topic. These are basic listening techniques you can use to improve your assertive communication skills.

Remember, for example, that paraphrasing is a good way to show the speaker that you've really listened. It will often foster a better understanding on your part, while also showing the speaker that you value what he or she is saying. When there's a natural pause in the conversation, state briefly what you heard your partner say by rephrasing in your own words. Then ask if this is correct.

Ask questions and request clarification of anything you don't quite understand. Asking people to explain their feelings helps draw them out to be more open and can help lead them to greater insight. Make sure you understand what you've heard before you react to what's been said. Remember, both you and the speaker are probably unaware of the subjective filtering process that takes place in your talk, so be sure to ask for clarification even when you don't think you really need it.

As you listen assertively, you should also be assertive about giving feedback. Feedback is simply telling the speaker your reaction to what you've heard. Make it clear that this feedback is based on your understanding of what has been said. If the feedback is negative in any way, be sure to add that your understanding might need adjustment. Always bear in mind three key rules for feedback in any business conversation: It must be immediate; it must be honest; and, while it can be negative in content, it must always be emotionally supportive and never mean-spirited or aggressive.

Be aware of body language. Up to 90 percent of interpersonal communication is visual. You're receiving not only words but also information through posture and what's called social distance (how close the other person is standing to you, and whether he is looking toward you or away from you). Most often body language prevails over words. Position yourself in a way that suggests empathy, openness, and attention. Nod your head occasionally as you listen, and maintain appropriate eye contact to show interest. Some people feel that nods and eye contact from the listener help them feel heard. Others find this body language distracting and prefer the listener to be still and attentive. Use your own judgment. Mirroring the speaker is a way of making that speaker feel comfortable. If you sense a discrepancy between what is explicitly being said and what you see, ask for clarification.

Be aware that interruptions, advice, or judgmental questions are all barriers to assertive listening. In the context of friendship or a personal conversation, relating a similar story to what you've heard is acceptable. But in a business conversation, it can be distracting and is usually an example of playing "topper." If you find yourself saying, "That reminds me of the time . . . ," resist the temptation to go on.

SINCERITY IS KEY

In any case, sincerity is the most crucial element in all human communication, whether as a speaker or a listener. Most people are able to accept a broad range of styles in a listener, provided that your attention is truly present and directed toward them. As an assertive listener, you must learn to validate every person's experience, regardless of your own beliefs or convictions. This doesn't mean that you have to agree with everyone. It does mean that you will hear and accept their impressions, letting go of your personal reactions and bringing attention always back to what's being said to you. This is a crucial people skill for all leaders.

At some point in the conversation, once a trusting relationship is well established, you can indicate that your own experience or that of others has led you to a different conclusion. But even as you do this, it's vital to stress at the same time that you hear the speaker's experience and the convictions that come from it. Don't feel that you have to elaborate on your own position in great detail. Even if you're asked to do so, it's a good idea to suggest that that might be the subject of another conversation, but that right now you'd prefer to listen to what your team member has to say. Very often, when a junior person asks for the manager to take over the conversation, it's really a way for the subordinate to back off and avoid confronting what he or she really wanted to say. Don't go for this gambit, even if the other person seems to want you to talk.

Assertive listening can be a transforming factor in the relationship between a leader and a team member. People who have felt threatened or devalued in the past can get the sense that they're truly unique and valuable, perhaps for the first time.

If conflict has developed, this can be a chance for both sides to learn about one another as colleagues, human beings, and even potential friends.

In general, our society doesn't teach assertive listening skills. We usually operate on a confrontational model of debate and reasoned argument, rather than on a model of listening carefully to everyone and arriving at mutual understanding and respect. Our paradigm is "the best idea will win," not "everyone has something to contribute to the best solution—which has probably not yet been thought of." It's important to note that both the confrontational model and that of assertive listening are searches for truth. They're simply different approaches. In terms of people skills, though, the combative approach will invariably leave someone behind and may well sow seeds for future conflict.

In this sense, assertive listening can be not only a peacemaking process but a peacekeeping process as well. It's been said that "an adversary is someone whose story we haven't heard yet."

Once you truly hear someone else's experience and understand their fears and aspirations, you will be unable to consider that person as anything but an ally. You may disagree with them, or even find their position directly contradictory to your own. But you will still see them as a contributor to a shared enterprise and as a valuable human being. As Dale Carnegie put it:

> *Thus you must learn to listen as well as to speak. Those who dismiss this as a mere platitude are already demonstrating an indisposition to listening: the phrase may be trite, but the message is hugely significant to your effectiveness as a leader. If you do not explicitly develop the skill of listening, you may not hear the secret which can launch you to fame and fortune.*

ACTION STEPS

1. It takes commitment and practice to be completely present and attentive to another when listening to them. Go through this list of conversation rules and mark an X or check beside any that you may need to work on. Once you have noted the areas that require more attention, practice them until they become part of your routine.

   ☐ I don't interrupt others or talk over them while they are speaking.

   ☐ I focus my attention completely on what the other is saying.

   ☐ I wait my turn to speak.

   ☐ I am an empathetic listener and make a point of trying to understand what others are trying to tell me.

☐   I support and encourage others when they speak.

☐   I do not compare myself to the speaker while they are talking.

☐   I avoid mind reading when listening to someone.

☐   I provide constructive feedback when spoken to.

☐   I am sincerely interested in others when they speak.

2. From a self-esteem perspective, it can be difficult to be an effective listener when we feel we need to be appreciated, heard, or recognized for the good work that we do. What three things can you do for yourself that will support your feeling that you've been heard and honored, so that you can be more present while in conversation with others?

3. At least once a day, make a commitment to be the listener during at least one conversation. Surrender your agenda and simply be present for the other individual. Then make note of any insights you may have developed while practicing this exercise.

ACTION PLAN NOTES

Reward, recognition, praise. It doesn't matter how you do it; what matters is that you do it again and again. Money is not the only effective reward, or even the most effective. Reward excellence. Encourage employee participation. Do this in ways that people appreciate.

—Dale Carnegie

CHAPTER 13

Assertive Ambition

Our topic here and in the following chapter is the fourth essential people skill, assertive ambition. At first glance, you might find that title somewhat redundant. After all, isn't ambition assertive by its very nature? Is it possible to be ambitious without being assertive?

Actually, assertiveness as we've defined it is not an inherent element of ambition. Remember: There's a difference between being assertive and being aggressive. An ambitious person may be very forceful and determined without being assertive in the true sense of the word. Aggressiveness often implies getting ahead at the expense of someone else. Assertiveness is a much more inner-directed concept. It's doing what you really want and getting what you really deserve. It includes other people doing the same.

With this in mind, let's make a distinction between what might be called intrinsic and extrinsic ambition. When people are extrinsically ambitious, their ambition is directed toward a target outside themselves—toward an external payoff or reward, and usually that reward is of a physical or material nature. The ambition of a new employee in a company, for example, might be to gain a specific title or to earn a certain amount of money within a certain number of years. But for an intrinsically ambitious person, the payoff is more emotional or even spiritual. It's a feeling of personal achievement or inner satisfaction that can't be touched or packaged. Ultimately it is more meaningful than a company car, a corner office, or even an expense account.

Here we will focus primarily on how you can develop assertive, intrinsic motivation in yourself. In chapter 14, we'll see how you can share and impart the principles to your team members. But whether we're talking about personal ambition or collective ambition for your whole organization, there are certain key ideas that you need to absorb. Some of them may surprise you.

We'll begin by looking at some very interesting things that have been learned about motivation and peak performance. Although these insights were gained through controlled studies (sometimes in laboratory settings), you'll quickly see how the information is transferable to the real world.

EXTERNAL REWARDS

You're probably aware, for example, that in laboratory experiments, animals can learn complex tasks when they're rewarded with a bite of peanut butter or breakfast cereal. In the same way, students are promised a grade of A for good work, and salespeople get larger commissions when they close more deals. It just stands to reason that external rewards promote better performance. This seems like a simple law of human nature.

And that's the problem. It's too simple. It's also wrong.

A growing body of research suggests that the benefits of traditional "rewards" are not as great as they might seem. Amazingly, social psychologists are finding that external rewards can actually lower performance levels. This becomes increasingly true over longer time frames, especially when the work involves creative thinking or initiating new ideas. Studies have also shown that intrinsic interest in a project (the sense that a task is worth doing for its own sake) generally declines when someone is externally rewarded for doing it. If an external reward such as money, praise, or a job promotion is the reason you're engaging in the activity, that activity will come to be seen as less worthwhile in its own right.

The implications of this research are truly startling. It suggests that the basic premises of performance and reward in the corporate environment may actually be discouraging to improvement and top achievement. The fact that rewards can have counterproductive effects is based on a variety of studies, and they've come up with such findings as these.

- Children who are rewarded for drawing are less likely to draw on their own than children who draw just for the fun of it.

- Teenagers offered rewards for playing word games enjoy the games less and do not do as well as those who play with no rewards.

- Employees who are praised for meeting a manager's expectations actually suffer a drop in motivation.

When one study asked a group of college students to invent imaginary movie plots, the students who had been contracted for rewards experienced greater difficulty. In similar research, a group of creative-writing students were asked to compose poetry. Some of them were given a list of external reasons for writing, such as impressing teachers, small amounts of money, or recommendations for graduate school. Others were given a list of intrinsic reasons: the enjoyment of playing with words, satisfaction from self-expression, and so forth. At the end of the study, the results were clear. Students given the extrinsic reasons not only wrote less creatively than the others (as judged by twelve independent poets) but the quantity of their work dropped significantly. Rewards, it seems, can have this kind of negative effect primarily with creative tasks, including higher-level problem solving. Findings show that the more complex the activity, the more it's hurt by extrinsic reward.

This research questions the widespread belief that money is an effective and even necessary way to motivate people. They also challenge the assumption that any goal is more likely to be achieved if it is rewarded. What is the logic behind these findings, and what do they tell us about how ambition should really be motivated?

WHY EXTRINSIC REWARDS DON'T WORK

First, rewards encourage people to focus narrowly on a task, to do it as quickly as possible, and to take few risks. If you feel that the task is something you have to get through to get the prize, you're going to be less creative, enthusiastic, and motivated.

Second, people come to see themselves as being controlled by the reward. They feel less in command, and this may interfere with performance. To the extent that your experience of being self-motivated is limited, your ambition will be reduced as well.

Finally, external rewards can erode intrinsic interest. People who see themselves as working for money, approval, or competitive success find their tasks less pleasurable, and therefore they don't do them as well. Money may work to "buy off" intrinsic motivation for an activity on a long-term basis. Research also shows that trying to beat others has the same effect. People who competed to solve a puzzle quickly were less likely than those who were not competing to keep working at it once the experiment was over.

There is general agreement, however, that not all rewards have the same effect. Offering a flat fee for participating in an experiment (similar to an hourly wage in the workplace) does not usually reduce intrinsic motivation. Problems develop, however, when the rewards are based on performing a given task or doing a good job at it. So the key lies in how a reward is experienced. If you come to view yourself as working to get something, you may no longer find that activity worth doing in its own right.

There's an important distinction to be made here, and it's a slightly subtle one. On the one hand, you can tell someone (or tell yourself) that you'll get a reward if you perform in a certain way. This is generally ineffective over the long term, as we've seen. But what about looking at what someone is already doing and rewarding the behaviors that are in the direction of the desired goals? For example, telling a team member that he'll get a bonus if he writes a good report is ineffective. It's much better to give him the tools and techniques to write a good report, and then giving him a bonus when he does so.

Any task, no matter how enjoyable it once seemed, is devalued if it's presented as a means rather than an end. For example, a group of volunteers were told they could not engage in an activity they liked until they first took part in another activity that they also enjoyed. Although they liked both activities equally, the subjects soon came to dislike the task that was a requirement before they could engage in the other.

There is a little story that illustrates this principle very nicely. Neighborhood children were harassing an elderly man, and he finally devised a scheme to put a stop to this. He offered to pay each child a dollar if they would all return on Tuesday and yell their insults at him again. The children were definitely surprised by this offer, but eagerly complied and received the money. As he paid them, however, the man had something more to say. He could pay them again for insulting him on Wednesday, but this time the rate would be only 25 cents per child. The kids were a bit disappointed, but they went along with the new rate. They returned on Wednesday and insulted him again. But then, as he handed out the quarters, the old man informed them that Thursday's payment would be just a penny. The kids were disgusted. "Forget about it!" they said, and they never taunted him again.

PRAISE AS A MEANS OF CONTROL

The principle that's working here isn't limited to money or other forms of physical reward. When praise or positive verbal feedback begins to be experienced as controlling, the effect on motivation can be similar to that of a financial payment. A study of corporate employees found that those who were told "Good job, you're doing just what you should be doing" were no more motivated than those who received only quantitative feedback.

There's a difference between saying "I'm giving you this reward because I personally recognize and appreciate your work" and saying "You are getting this reward because you've met certain standards." The first is a personal, human interaction. It's an example of assertive people skills. This ignites assertive ambition, both in the person who hears it and the person who says it.

The negative impact on motivation through reward can be minimized by playing down the significance of these rewards and trying not to use them in a controlling way. You can't force ambition or motivation, but you can create an environment in which those qualities can take root and flourish.

A DEFINITION OF AMBITION

In simplest terms, ambition can be defined as wanting to achieve something that is desired or planned. In more poetic terms, it is having a dream and experiencing success when that dream is attained. Your ambition is rewarded when your dreams come true.

Exactly what makes up those dreams varies from one person to another. Dreams are a subjective experience, and so is the ambition that moves us toward them. They can take as many different forms as there are different human beings in a family, a company, or even in the world. In a similar way, the feelings that work against ambition are also subjective and individual. For our purposes here, however, we're going to identify those feelings by one word. Then we're going to look more closely at what that word represents, in order to minimize its effect on our lives. As a leader working with a team of diverse individuals, it's very important to grasp the multifaceted meanings of this word, to identify how the meanings express themselves in your team members, and to work consistently to eliminate them.

What is this single word that represents the polar opposite of assertive ambition? The one word that always pulls the plug on motivation and achievement in a business setting? The word is *fear*.

DEALING WITH FEAR

As we've tried to show, ambition is a subjective experience and so is the fear that works against it. Still, there are certain very important points that should be made about fear; insights about how it begins, how it works, and how it can be eliminated. Generally speaking, there are four factors that give rise to fear. Let's take a look at those factors right now.

As a leader, you've probably noticed that there are basically two different categories of employees. There are people who can do several things well and who have the potential to move up in the company in a number of different directions. A team member might be good at sales, for example, and perhaps that person is also good in human resources and customer service. While they are related fields, they're also different from one another in a number of respects. Then there's another kind of team member whom we can call a specialist, as opposed to the kind of generalist we've just been speaking of. These are people who are very good at accounting, for instance, but they really aren't comfortable doing anything else. They like the sense of mastery and control that comes from working in their specialty. They can be very ambitious individuals, but their ambition will follow a specific path in an organization. A very good accountant can become a very good chief financial officer, but nobody's interests would be served by moving that person into human resources.

In short, people generally fall into two main categories: those who really excel at one thing, and others, who are good at many things although perhaps not truly outstanding at any of them. A good leader should be very reluctant to believe that some individuals simply aren't good at anything. Everyone has a strength of some kind. The unfortunate thing is, not all of us recognize what that strength is, either in ourselves or in the people around us. Over the long term, few of us capitalize to the greatest possible degree on our real strength.

The cause of this can be a lack of self-understanding, a lack of focus on who you really are, or a lack of awareness or acknowledgment of what you really do well. It's a form of fear, because it is usually based on trying to live up to what you think you're supposed to be, instead of being who you are. It's trying to be a different kind of person than you really are. In terms of ambition, it's aspiring to the wrong thing at the basic level of your own identity.

The Successful Specialist

Among people who are specialists, the most successful individuals recognize this quality early on. They see what they're good at and what they enjoy doing, and they channel their careers in that direction. Their ambition asserts itself in a way that's congruent with their essential nature. They pursue the right major in school, for example. They go to work for companies that have a need for their particular skills, and they seek out mentors who can help them develop their inherent strength. Their key to success is that they focus ambition in the best possible direction. For a specialist, the danger lies in being afraid of admitting what that direction really is. If you are a specialist, your ambition should be channeled within a parameter that you must be very reluctant to violate.

The Winning Generalist

Conversely, some people are gifted at many things, but they turn that strength into an area of vulnerability. It's good to be a generalist, but it's not good to spread yourself too thin. Many generalists allocate their resources to a variety of areas but might not make a strong impact in any particular area. If you're a multitalented individual of this kind, don't be afraid to focus your ambition. When you're working in a particular area, don't become distracted or attracted by something else. Focus on one area at a time. Ideally this should be an area in which your skill will allow you to really take off. It should be an area that can help you achieve your future goals and that will assert your ambition in the larger context of your organization. When you can do that, you'll become successful not only in terms of your place in the company but also in the eyes of the most important judge of all—yourself.

So, to sum up this first category of fear that impedes ambition, it's fear of recognizing who you are, what kind of talent you have, and making the most of it.

Fear Disguised as Impatience

A second kind of fear manifests itself as impatience. It's being afraid to take the time to develop your abilities, and therefore very quickly either giving up or getting in over your head. This is something that happens very frequently in the corporate environment, and it's especially common among very ambitious people. You want to get ahead as quickly as possible. When you see an opening, your instinct is to go for it, even if you know in your heart that you're not really ready.

A very interesting study in this area focused on army parachute training. Among every group of recruits, there were a certain number who froze at the doorway of the aircraft when it came time to make their first jump. Generally these were not soldiers who had shown any indication of trouble during their previous training. On the contrary, they were usually people who had done very well and who were very ambitious about succeeding in this area of the military. And as it turned out, that was really the problem. In their own minds, the people who froze at the door had never confronted the possibility that they might freeze. Their confidence on the surface was so high that they couldn't acknowledge the vulnerability that lay underneath. They moved ahead too quickly, in the sense that they overlooked what was really going on in their minds and hearts. By not recognizing the presence of fear, they set themselves up for an overwhelming experience of fear at the critical moment.

The second kind of fear, therefore, is fear of recognizing the areas in yourself that still need work. That kind of fear uses ambition to cover itself. It says, "Don't waste any more time on preparation. You've got to get ahead as quickly as possible." The problem is that if you try to get ahead too quickly, you're almost certainly going to fall behind.

We've just been discussing a certain kind of pressure: the pressure that comes from impatience and the fear that prevents you from taking the time to develop real self-understanding. Pressure can also express itself as other kinds of fear, however. Suppose, for example, that you're a very ambitious manager and a very effective one as well. You're moving up in the company. You go from one level to the next, and the responsibilities keep getting bigger. There's added pressure at each stage, but you tell yourself you can take it, until one day it all becomes too much.

Fear Under Pressure

What's really happened here? Internally, perhaps at a subconscious level, a fear of taking on more responsibility has always been present. The added pressure scared you, but you didn't want to get in touch with that. You wanted to make ambition, pure and simple, the defining quality of your being. But that's aggressive ambition, not assertive ambition. Assertively ambitious leaders accurately assess their careers and themselves. Based on that assessment, sometimes they take on additional pressure and sometimes they don't. People who crash and burn might think that the choice is only between being a leader or a follower. They may think a leader is somebody who never flinches. If that sounds like you, you're telling yourself you're not afraid of one thing, when you're really afraid of something else. What's more, you're ignoring the thing that really scares you.

So this third kind of fear is about pressure. It's not only about taking on too much pressure but about being afraid to admit that there's even such a thing as too much.

Fear of Seeing Your Limits

Don't ignore the fact that you can be an assertively ambitious and highly successful leader without wanting to be the CEO of a Fortune 100 company. You can want to lead without wanting to lead everybody. You can still be a hugely influential person even if one or two people are even more influential than you are. There's nothing wrong with this. Assertive ambition means wanting success however you choose to define it. But don't be afraid to admit that you have limits or that you even want to have limits. That doesn't mean you aren't ambitious, it just means that you're ambitious on your own terms.

Let's use an example from the world of sports to illustrate this. In the early 1970s, Pete Maravich was the greatest college

basketball player in America. Growing up as the son of a basketball coach, he was schooled to be a pro from early childhood.
He dribbled a basketball wherever he went. He dribbled it when
he was riding a bicycle, when he was eating his lunch, and even
when he was lying in bed. By the time he was a collegiate player
at Louisiana State University, he was scoring at least 40 points
every game, and he often scored 50 or 60. Of course, that was
only the preamble to what he had really been preparing for, which
was the National Basketball Association. Once he got to the NBA,
there couldn't be any drop-off. He created an internal mind-set in
which he had to score 40 or 45 points every night, and he had also
created that expectation in his fans. Of course, he was now facing
the greatest players in the world, but that didn't mean he could
be any less productive than he was against high school players or
collegians. Pete had put himself into a very difficult position. If he
didn't score twice as many points as any other player in the game,
he considered himself a failure, and everybody else did as well.

This is an example of the fourth kind of ambition-related fear.
It's fear of seeing what your limits really are or that you even
have them in the first place. The fact is that everybody has limits.
There's no dishonor in seeing that yours may be slightly different from the next person's, especially when the only thing that
prevents you from doing so is fear of seeing that reality. It doesn't
mean that you're any less ambitious. It just means that you're
ready to assert what's true about yourself.

RESPECTING YOURSELF AND OTHERS

In a business environment, respect is a very important concept.
It's a mistake to measure respect in terms of how much others
respect you. Instead, focus on how respectful you are to your team
members and how much respect you have for yourself. When you
do this, you'll realize that the respect you show to others will be
returned to you. This is especially true in the corporate world,
where it may seem that your goal is to blow past everybody or

even to walk right over anyone who gets in your way. In terms of ambition and people skills in general, this aggressive approach is a mistake. If the objective is to make it to the top, it's easier getting there when others are supporting you or even pushing you, not when you're stepping on them every chance you get.

This is such a key point. Even if you're a hugely aggressive manager and you make it to the top, your job will be a lot easier if your team members are there to support you. How good will you look if everybody bails out on you?

If you're genuinely bright, talented, and ambitious, fear not. You'll be noticed. There's no need to blow your own horn, much less to do so at the expense of anyone else. In fact, praising everyone around you is an excellent way to be assertively ambitious. A leader is most effective when he empowers others to do well.

It's not really a matter of being a sweet person or a mean person, of being a good cop or a bad cop. Instead of thinking in terms of good or bad, think in terms of trust or lack of trust, and trust in yourself most of all. These are not easy concepts to grasp. It's so tempting to mistake mere aggressiveness for assertive ambition. Greed and insensitivity are strong psychological forces that are amplified in business. By turning away from those temptations, you may pass up on some short-term gains. Ultimately, though, you'll reap the trust of others and gain the long-term prize.

In the next chapter, we'll continue our discussion of assertive ambition with an emphasis on how you can maximize it in your team members.

ACTION STEPS

1. Surprising evidence revealed that external encouragement toward people of various ages did not prove to be effective. They were driven more by internal factors. Can you think of a personal example where promising you a reward did not help motivate you but actually demotivated you? What are some activities you do for the intrinsic value?

2. Some research argues that when you receive monetary or other rewards for the work that you do, you can actually be demotivated. Reflect back on your life. Have you ever had a hobby of other area of expertise that you excelled in but ultimately did not want to turn into a business? Perhaps you turned a passion into a business, then found yourself no longer enjoying the activity. Write about any such revelations that you or someone you know has had.

3. Genuine praise carries a great deal more weight than praise that is spoken with manipulation in mind. Take note of when you praise others, and stop yourself, if possible, before you make any statement. Ask yourself what your intentions are. If your praises are sincere and in no way a manipulation, go ahead. If, however you discover that you are using the praise as a means toward an end in your personal agenda, refrain from making any comments. Write about your findings and any insights you may have discovered.

ACTION PLAN NOTES

When dealing with people, let us remember we are not dealing with creatures of logic. We are dealing with creatures of emotion, creatures bustling with prejudices and motivated by pride and vanity.

—Dale Carnegie

CHAPTER 14

Maximizing Results with Assertive Ambition

I n this chapter we'll continue our discussion of assertive ambition with an emphasis on how you as a leader can maximize the positive energy of ambition for everyone on your team.

LEAD BY EXAMPLE

In the past twenty years, there has been an explosion of books and audio programs on effective management. Dale Carnegie was one of the pioneers who set this process in motion. Today the Dale Carnegie's success-building principles are more relevant than ever before, and if there's one idea that continues to stand out, it's "lead by example."

Amid the thousands of leadership tools and techniques, the notion that you must "walk the talk" still stands above the rest. It doesn't matter whether you're the coach of a professional football team, the head of a multinational corporation, or the parent of a growing family. Every great leader knows this secret and puts it to use every moment of every day.

Leading by example not only instructs your team members but also inspires them to achieve greater results. In this way it ignites assertive ambition. If you show what needs to happen instead of just talking about it, you and your team will reach your objective much more quickly. This can present a problem for a leader who would rather have people "do as I say and not as I do." It doesn't matter what you want others to do. If you're not willing to set the example first, you will be ineffective. Ultimately, if you're really interested in improving the performance of your team members, the message has to come from the top down.

THE MODEL LEADER

Here's an example of what this means. When Mike was named the new head of his company's marketing department, he knew he had his work cut out for him. The results in that department had been slowly decreasing, and the drop in results was crippling the company's ability to improve and expand. Mike was assertively ambitious about improving that situation, and he wanted to kindle that same ambition throughout his team.

Before he stepped into his new role, Mike had been given a quick overview of the problem. Basically, the sales force was failing to meet reasonable expectations. If things didn't improve fast, Mike was to remove the current employees and hire a new team. This was a very sobering thought. Mike understood that things needed to get better—not just for his sake but for the sake of all the people working for him.

Based on his knowledge of the marketing department before he took over, Mike knew what the difficulty was. Very simply, the previous head of the department had not been providing the right kind of leadership. There wasn't a problem with the team as a whole. They were just echoing the message that they were being given, which was that talk was a worthy substitute for action.

By working as hard as he wanted others to work, Mike quickly improved the morale of the team. He let them know that he would never ask more of them than he did of himself. He showed up early, worked with focus and intent, and stayed late. He made it clear that he had high ambitions for the department, and he wanted others to feel the same way. Mike made himself the example, and he invited the team members to follow his lead.

In only a few weeks the marketing department looked like a completely different group. They were excited about their work, committed to their goals, and ambitious about their future. Results quickly improved and they were on their way to breaking company records.

What would have happened if everyone in the marketing department had been replaced in an attempt to solve the problem? The answer is that nothing would have happened—not unless there was a change in the leadership style of the department head. What was missing was not talented workers but the right kind of example for them to follow. When things began to turn around, the team members hadn't changed, but the leadership and the expectations had.

This is the single most important principle for building assertive ambition in your team. Pay less attention to what you say to people and more attention to what you do. If there's something you want to see in others, make sure they can see it in you first.

Now, keeping that first crucial principle in mind, we can look at some other very powerful techniques you can use to instill assertive ambition in your team members—and thereby get maximum performance from them both today and over the long term.

THE FIRST FEW MINUTES OF THE DAY ARE KEY

For example, be aware that the first few minutes of the day are always the most important time you'll have with your team. You can set the tone for the rest of the day, inspiring everyone to achieve greater results, or you can lead them without ambition or energy. It's your choice.

Recognizing the importance of getting each day off to a great start, here are four specific tactics for making that happen.

TACTIC 1: *Arrive Early*

First, arrive early. There's nothing quite as frustrating to employees as seeing their supervisor, manager, or leader strolling in hours after the workday has begun. It's very difficult to respect leaders who fail to give as much as they expect in return, especially when it's something as basic as getting to work on time. So arrive at work before or with your team members, and let that action demonstrate your ambition for them, for yourself, and for the company.

TACTIC 2: *Keep Your Energy High*

Second, keep your energy level high. Moods and attitudes are contagious. The moment you first walk through the door, you're sending out all sorts of messages. These messages are relayed by what you say, by how you're dressed, and even by how you stand or walk. You can slump your shoulders and drag your way into the office and you'll let everyone around you know that the day is going to be long and uneventful. If you walk in with a spring in your step and a smile on your face, however, you'll bring the enthusiasm that will initiate a productive workday. Everyone has a vibe, and as a leader, your vibe can often influence that of your team members. So use this power to enhance the quality of each day.

TACTIC 3: *Greet Your Team with Enthusiasm and Humor*

Third, make it a habit to meet and greet your team with enthusiasm and good humor. Making this a personal goal is a great way to display assertive ambition as a leader. If there's one key difference between leaders who inspire ambition and those who stifle it, it's the direction they head when they first come to work in the morning. Some choose to walk straight to their own office or work area. Others take a more interactive path, and this quickly pays off with improved morale and productivity.

So start the day by greeting your team members. In this way, you can let them know through your actions that you see them as important assets to the company. If you just run to your office and don't acknowledge people around you, you can only undermine the success of those who are relying on you for leadership.

TACTIC 4: *Have a Clear Action Plan*

The fourth point is most directly connected to our theme of assertive ambition. It concerns the level of expectations you have for your team members. Communicating these expectations can be done very simply. Just have a clear plan of action for what needs to be accomplished every day. Share that plan with your team when you speak with them each morning.

People need direction. They need to know where they are heading and why. So, as you greet your employees, let them know what results you expect to see by the end of the day and how they will benefit. Relaying clear ambitions and expectations each morning will point the day in the right direction. The key to this, of course, is to make your presence felt in a proactive and positive manner. Avoid positioning yourself as a boss in the old-fashioned sense, or as a taskmaster. As always, be confident and assertive rather than aggressive or passive. Most important, though, is to be there.

LAZINESS

Along with our discussion of assertive ambition, it would be a mistake not to take a quick look at the opposite of ambition, and that's laziness. To ignore the reality of lazy people in the workplace would be like refusing to acknowledge the presence of an elephant in the conference room. Lazy people are everywhere. They are people who are going half speed, three-quarter speed, or maybe at no speed at all. Bringing this issue into the open isn't being negative. It's just being honest. It's recognizing what's out there so it can be dealt with effectively.

Laziness, like everything else, has become more sophisticated in the twenty-first century. Lazy people have several tricks to make it look as if they're actually accomplishing something. One of the most common might be called a "woolly mammoth." During the Ice Age, primitive hunters and gatherers longed to find an animal that was so big and laden with meat that the entire tribe could live off it for a year—the woolly mammoth. But woolly mammoths also exist in the modern workplace. They're rare, but if a lazy person can find one, it's worth its weight in gold. You see, when a lazy person does something right, they love sitting on their success until it turns to stone. When they do something good, they take it to mean that they don't have to do anything else for a few months. That's the beauty of a woolly mammoth.

The problem is, lazy people themselves suffer the real loss. You can find a secure niche in an organization just by treading water, but you can never really move up. In the end, though, nothing is more difficult and draining than being bored all the time. And there's nothing more depressing.

An amazing illustration of this principle came out of the Korean War in the early 1950s. When the North Korean forces captured a group of American troops, the Americans were offered a choice. If they signed a paper that accused the United States of war crimes and spoke highly of the enemy cause, their captivity would turn into a life of luxury. They could have whatever they wanted. They would be in no danger, and nothing they asked for would be denied. On the other hand, troops who refused to sign the paper would have to live in the worst possible conditions. They would be in constant fear for their lives, and they would be allowed only a bare minimum of food and water. Despite these threats, very few American troops agreed to cooperate with the North Koreans. But a few did agree to cooperate, with surprising results. Although their living conditions could not have been more different, the health of the turncoats very quickly declined. Some took their own lives, and many suffered from what today would be called clinical depression. Whereas those who had not opted for the easy way out seemed somehow to find energy and strength in the difficulties they faced, and the percentage of survival among these troops was much higher than for the others.

This reveals a very important point. Success isn't just a matter of being comfortable. On the contrary, real success seems to demand a certain amount of discomfort. We need something to strive for. We want something to struggle against. We long for something toward which we can direct our ambition. In the absence of it, we may think we'll be satisfied, but in truth we may become complacent and disappointed.

So when you encounter laziness in one of your team members, don't be hesitant about confronting it and pointing out its dangers. This is what's best for the organization, and it's also best for the individual in question. The person may feel hurt or angry at first, but in the end they'll thank you.

FAILURE AS A POSITIVE SIGN

Even if you do a great job of imbuing your team with assertive ambition, however, there will be times when things don't work out exactly as everyone had hoped. You should not only expect this but actually look forward to it. Why? If there isn't a certain amount of so-called failure among your team members, the sights probably haven't been set high enough. In other words, there hasn't been enough assertive ambition.

Let's look more closely at exactly what this means. You should not invite failure. Some falling short of brilliant success, however, will awaken you to the fact that millions of great ideas go to waste each year. It's in your interest as a leader to make sure that your team wastes as few as possible. As a step in that direction, be aware of the thought processes in the minds of today's corporate employees. Face the fact that the minds of your team members are a battleground, a territory in which negative and positive energies are constantly at war. Your job is to make sure that the positive side wins!

This positive energy is nothing other than the natural ambition of every human being to be successful. Each new day presents new opportunities to grow, learn, and progress beyond where they were the day before. Success means something different to each person, but the underlying idea of achieving dreams and goals excites and inspires us all.

The drive for success and achievement is powerful, but sometimes a negative force can battle it to a standstill. If left to its own devices, this negative force can win the war in a split second. What makes it especially dangerous is the fact that you can't really put your finger on it. By its very nature, it hides behind the scenes.

FEAR OF FAILURE

What is it? The negative force in your team members can be simply the fear of failure. It's not anything that they do. It's what they're afraid of doing. On an individual level, this fear stifles their ambition to assert their ideas in the world. Collectively, it erases a source of innovation that could improve the performance of the company. It drives people to keep still, keep quiet, and keep potentially great thoughts locked away forever.

Allowing the negative force of fear to dominate a team member's workday robs both the team member and the company of something very valuable. It's not so much the result that could come from taking a chance on the new initiative. It's taking the chance as an end in itself. Sure, there will be many times when nothing comes of sticking your neck out. In fact, most of the time nothing will come of it. On occasion it may even cost the organization some money. However, the surest way to long-term failure is not risking failure in the short term.

So which force will win the day in the minds of your team members? The answer is really up to you. It depends on the energy and atmosphere you create in your team, and especially in yourself. Conventional wisdom might counsel avoiding failure at all cost, but assertively ambitious leaders expect and welcome it.

A quick example can clarify this. Suppose your team deals with a hundred clients and every one of them is perfectly satisfied. What could be better? You're batting a thousand, aren't you? Well, not exactly. Because what have you learned? What have you gained from those one hundred customers that can help you reach the thousands of customers whom you've never met? Almost certainly, you have no clue as to why the experience of the satisfied customers was positive. You just know that they transacted their business and moved on without a complaint. That's very good in the short term, but what new opportunities is it opening up?

Let's suppose your team decides to try something new. It could be a new product or service or a new way of making them affordable to your customers. In any case, suppose it doesn't work. Customers are unhappy. They're complaining like mad. True, this represents failure in one sense, but in the big picture you're being offered success on a silver platter. The angry customers are telling you exactly what you can do to improve your business. No guessing, no assuming. You're getting specific instructions on how *not* to do something, which is a big step in the direction of learning to do it right. These angry people are pointing to vast, uncharted territories. Now you and your team just need the ambition to go there.

When you give team members the freedom to try new things, to take chances, and even to accept a reasonable risk of failure, you will be amazed by the abundance of ideas that start arising. And some of them will work. Once again, most of them won't, but a single big hit can make up for many misses. If you do the math, you'll see that the odds are in your favor when you back some long shots. In fact, some of the most successful innovations come from lower-level employees who are given the chance to be heard. If you create an atmosphere in which 100 percent success is demanded at every stage of the game, you'll short-circuit the ambition on which success and achievement really depend.

Looking again at our example of the angry customers, you not only get more ideas when you allow for short-term failure but also gain access to a detailed road map for success. When a team member fails, take steps to learn everything that's available from that experience. This is valuable information. When you know why something didn't work, you're not far from learning how it can and will.

CREATING ASSERTIVE AMBITION WITHIN YOUR TEAM

When we speak about creating assertive ambition in your team members, we need to make a distinction between theory and practice. It's easy to see why it's better to have an ambitious team than a complacent one. In practice, though, what specifically can you do to make that happen? To answer that question, let's look at a three-step process that you can put into action starting today.

CREATING A CULTURE OF LEARNING

The first step is creating a culture of learning in your team. Create a program that consistently brings in the latest trends, research, techniques, and tools of your industry. You could, for example, assign a different team member each day to share something he or she has learned. It could be sourced from professional journals, internet websites, or hands-on experience in the workplace.

This will satisfy a very strong and very human need in your team members. It will answer to their need to learn and grow. Education is really a zero-sum game. If you're not learning new things, it's not just that you'll be standing still. You'll actually be falling behind, and fast, because new concepts and ideas are coming into play at a furious pace. You've got to stay in touch with them in order to keep up.

Countless resources exist to help with this process of ongoing education. Purchasing books and magazines is one of the easiest steps you can take. You can create a library in your workplace, or you can just have them lying around for people to glance at when they have a moment. Education doesn't have to take place in a formal academic setting, and books don't have to stay on bookshelves in order to be read. In fact, they probably shouldn't stay there.

The next step is a little more time-consuming and expensive, but it too is hugely worthwhile. Send your team members to live seminars or training programs. They'll come back with a heightened sense of professionalism and a wealth of new information. Needless to say, you should also attend these events yourself as often as you possibly can. Being an assertively ambitious leader means that you have to know your industry backward and forward. You should always be on top of where it's been, where it is, and where it's going. Don't expect team members to get to that level of professionalism until you've gotten there yourself.

The third step relates to what you do with the ideas and information that have been learned. Any time or money you spend on education is wasted unless the lessons are put to use. Millions of dollars are spent each year to further the education, training, and development of employees, but upon returning to their companies, the ideas are soon forgotten. The investment was a waste. To prevent that from happening, you'll need to create an atmosphere in which the new ideas your people learn are valued and shared. As always, this is really just a matter of being assertive. Get your team together and ask them about what they've learned. Find out how they think this information can improve the company. Have them share with the rest of the team the information they learned. There is potential success in their ideas, but you're the one who has to bring it to the surface.

While not every idea will pan out, actually trying new things is the greatest benefit of employee education. The process doesn't end there, however. Even if your company improves in the short term because of the new information, the greater benefit will be a long-term one. The type of team member whom ongoing education, training, and development create will far outweigh any monetary costs that you incur.

Think about how you would feel if you went to a seminar on reducing employee turnover, and when you returned to your company, you were never asked about what you learned. You were excited about the chance to grow. You learned some really useful ideas that would fit well with your organization, but everything you've done is wasted.

The situation would be so different if your supervisor had eagerly awaited your return, anxious to hear your ideas. You would feel needed, important, and ambitious toward the future.

By understanding how you would feel in that situation, you can grasp how your team members feel also. Trying out new ideas is a way of giving everyone a chance to move the organization forward. If your team is already being given opportunities to learn and grow, you're headed in the right direction. If they are not, there are some changes that need to be made right away.

EACH CASE IS UNIQUE

Before we close our discussion of assertive ambition, there's one more point that needs to be made loudly and clearly. It's one thing to say that everyone should be productive and ambitious and that you should do everything possible to foster productivity. The real meaning of assertive ambition, however, can be entirely different from one person to another.

Far too many people in positions of management or leadership try to motivate their teams using a "one size fits all" approach. The people on your team are as different as baked beans and apple pie. They each need an individual form of motivation, and it's up to you to discover what that is in every case. What turns them on? What turns them off? It may take a little time and effort on your part, but uncovering the powerful motivators that drive your people will be the best thing you can do for you and your team. Be assertively ambitious about making that discovery!

ACTION STEPS

1. Do an honest review of your life. Do you always "walk the talk"? Where and when have your actions not matched your words? Make a list of the areas in your life where your words or actions are not consistent with your values. Once you have created that list, make a commitment to yourself and your team to model your messages.

2. In the example of Mike, as a leader he was held responsible for the performance of his team. Reflect on your leadership skills and make a list of at least three things that you can do to further motivate your team and boost morale, productivity, and initiative.

3. Listed below are the four leadership tactics. For the next week, go down this list and check that you have used all tactics to enlist the enthusiasm and productivity of your team.

☐ ☐ ☐ ☐ ☐   Tactic 1: Arrive early

☐ ☐ ☐ ☐ ☐   Tactic 2: Keep your energy high

☐ ☐ ☐ ☐ ☐   Tactic 3: Greet your team with enthu-
                                siasm and humor

☐ ☐ ☐ ☐ ☐   Tactic 4: Have a clear action plan

ACTION PLAN NOTES

You can make more friends in a month by trying to get interested in other people than you can in two years by trying to get other people interested in you.

—Dale Carnegie

CHAPTER 15

Assertive Conflict Resolution

We've now come a long way in our discussion of people skills and how they can be assertively put into action. There are only two chapters left in the book, and they are equally practical and important. The first takes us to the fifth and final essential people skill, assertive conflict resolution. Conflict is a reality in the workplace and it's essential that leaders learn tools to effectively deal with and resolve issues before they escalate. There are many reasons for this. Legal issues around conflict have come to the fore. Expensive court fees have become the consequence of what used to be merely unpleasant incidents. This is especially true when the conflict erupts around issues of race, gender, age, ethnicity, or many other sensitive areas. Most disturbing, there have been well-publicized incidents in which workplace conflicts have turned violent. All these factors have made conflict prevention and resolution tools more valuable than ever before.

At the outset, let's get a perspective on exactly what's involved in these kinds of situations and on how complicated they can become. To do that, we'll look at an incident from the life of a man who is better known for things other than getting into fights. As you'll see, his esteemed reputation came later in his career.

LINCOLN'S VALUABLE LESSON ON CONFLICT RESOLUTION

In 1842, Abraham Lincoln was thirty-two years old and serving his third term in the Illinois state legislature. Lincoln had already acquired a reputation as a hardworking lawyer, something of an athlete, and a gifted teller of humorous stories. He also had a habit of writing editorials and letters to the editor of his local newspaper. Often these were laced with self-deprecating jokes at his own expense. Not always, though. Sometimes Mary Todd, his future wife, helped him compose his submissions to the newspaper, and these collaborations tended to have a more aggressive kind of wit. Usually Lincoln and Mary used the pseudonym Rebecca to sign their letters.

In the spring of 1842 Lincoln wrote a letter to the newspaper that explicitly attacked another state official named James Shields. This individual was not exactly a popular man about town. He was widely viewed as a braggart and a loudmouth. In his letter, Lincoln used a satirical style to attack Shields for his political views, and he also called Shields a liar and a coward. Strangely, after the first letter appeared, three more followed in rapid succession, all of them attacking Shields. Shields was outraged. He demanded to know who had written all these letters signed with the name Rebecca. Of course, Lincoln was puzzled too, but he soon found out that Mary Todd and a friend of hers were the culprits.

In order to protect the identities of the women, Lincoln took responsibility for all of the letters, but Shields was by no means satisfied. In fact, he challenged Lincoln to a duel. Lincoln had no choice but to accept, but this marked a real turning point in what today would be called his people skills.

Lincoln realized that he had been making a tremendous mistake with his provocative letters. Although Shields was indeed an extremely unpleasant character, it was clear to Lincoln that he himself had provoked this conflict, and now he was going to have to fight a duel over it. According to the rules of dueling, it was up to Lincoln to choose the weapons. Since Shields was only five feet nine and Lincoln was six feet four, Lincoln sought to maximize his height advantage by selecting extremely long cavalry swords. Before the duel actually took place, however, Lincoln wrote one more letter. He wrote a letter to Shields himself. In this letter, Lincoln offered to print a public apology to Shields in the newspaper. For a man who was already a public figure with high political ambitions, this was a bold step. Lincoln knew that he had caused the conflict and that it was his responsibility to resolve it, even if it meant losing face. Shields, however, refused to accept Lincoln's offer, and the duel took place as scheduled.

Fortunately, as the duel began, Shields quickly realized that Lincoln's long reach created a hopeless mismatch. Lincoln made this clear by reaching over Shields's head with his sword and cutting off a branch of a tree. At this point friends of both men intervened and the duel came to an end. So did the conflict. The men shook hands and returned to their homes. Lincoln had learned something very important, however, and he never again wrote an anonymous letter. He never again directed his wit at another person in public. Years later, he acknowledged that the Shields incident was one of the most painful memories of his life. Without doubt, it was also one of the most important memories. With the lessons that he learned from it, he was later able to find compassion and respect for the Southern states after their defeat in the Civil War. This momentous event likely played a significant role in his refusal to enact the harsh punishments that many recommended. It's worth noting too that during the war Lincoln asked his old enemy Shields to serve as a general in the Union Army.

In discussing workplace conflicts and how you can assertively resolve them, we'll make a distinction between two kinds of situations. The first are those in which you are directly involved as one of the parties in conflict, and the second are conflicts in which you are a third party or mediator.

PARTICIPATING IN A CONFLICT

When you are directly involved in a conflict as one of the participants, there are certain assertive steps that you can and should take as soon as possible. As we look at these one by one, please notice that none of them depends on the specific issues around which the conflict is taking place. None of them focuses on determining who is right or wrong, or who is good or bad. In the worst-case scenario, lawyers or professional mediators can decide those questions. For our purposes, however, we'll simply assume that angry conflict in a business setting is inherently negative and unproductive. Our goal will be to assertively bring it to an end as quickly and as fairly as possible.

In looking at any conflict situation, a good place to start is by identifying the variables. These are the places where there's a real possibility for change or adjustment. When you're one of the principals in a conflict, you'll sometimes see many of these areas and sometimes very few. Some elements in the conflict are always amenable to change, and these are your own thoughts, feelings, and responses. Even when the other side in a conflict seems totally unwilling to change, you can still exert a positive influence. It's up to you to do so. True, your ego can get in the way, but being flexible to some extent doesn't mean you have to let other people walk all over you. This is just another instance where you can choose assertiveness over aggressiveness or passivity. Let's look at some specific elements in making that choice.

MAKE AN HONEST ASSESSMENT

First, make an honest assessment of the power balance in the specific situation. One of the hard things about business conflict is the fact that it quickly becomes totally unsentimental. When money and workplace issues are involved, it's amazing how quickly everything else burns away. All the lunches, the company retreats, and the softball games mean nothing when the pedal meets the metal in a corporate setting. Ironically, this is something that makes business conflicts easier to handle than serious arguments between spouses, family members, or close friends. In those conflicts, there really are deep emotional issues that can make a clear resolution very difficult to come by. In business arguments, you may be shocked to realize how little personal feelings mean when push comes to shove.

Steve Makes an Honest Assessment

As you examine the power balance in the conflict, look at the difference between what the parties merely want and what they really need. Here's an example of what this means. Steve was a human resources expert. He created roundtable meetings in which corporations could hear experts speak about HR issues, and where information could be exchanged. Steve organized an average of one roundtable a month at sites in the United States, the Pacific Rim countries, and Western Europe. It was very important to Steve's business that these events take place in first-class hotels, with excellent dining and accommodations. It was also important that the guest speakers be recognized authorities in the field. Steve was very good at making this happen, and his business was very successful for more than twenty years.

More recently, it came to Steve's attention that his website needed to be updated to match the other aspects of his events. Steve had had a website for a number of years, but he had never paid much attention to it. The website was just one of several ways in which potential clients could get information about the business or current clients could find out about upcoming events. When a client mentioned that Steve's website looked embarrassingly outdated, he began to search for a first-rate website designer.

Steve interviewed a number of people, and before long he found Sharon, who seemed to have exactly the capabilities that he needed. There was only one problem. When Sharon told Steve about her fee, his jaw just about hit the floor. The very idea of paying that much money for website design seemed outrageous. Sharon, however, pointed out that hers was a reasonable market price for a top-notch designer. According to her, this was what Steve would have to pay if he wanted outstanding work. He could pay less, of course, but he would also get less than the optimum result.

Although Steve and Sharon had gotten along well in their initial discussions, it was amazing how quickly their negotiations grew hostile. To Steve, it almost seemed impertinent of Sharon to suddenly grow so demanding when she had been so friendly up to this point. On a purely emotional level, he wanted nothing more to do with her.

If Steve got rid of Sharon, however, where would he be? Sharon was telling the truth when she said that hers was the going rate for good web designers. When he took the emotion out of it, Steve saw that he needed exactly what Sharon offered. On the other hand, what he wanted was something very different. He desired a first-rate designer who would charge much less money. In the real world, though, after additional research on the part of Steve, it seemed that this wasn't possible. In any case, he would certainly have to do a lot more interviewing. What's more, Steve actually did have the financial resources to pay what Sharon was asking. In truth, the basis of the conflict was the fact that Steve felt personally insulted by what Sharon was asking. Once he took those feelings out of the equation and looked at the business realities, it was easy to close the deal with Sharon. This was not backing down. This was assertive conflict resolution, which includes being assertive with yourself as well as the other party.

So an honest, nuts-and-bolts assessment of the situation, including your needs, is the first step toward resolving it. Making this assessment is your responsibility, but it's not your only responsibility in assertive conflict resolution. You also need to give the other side whatever information is necessary for them to make a decision and reach the same level of clarity that you have.

In the situation we just looked at, Sharon did a good job. She was clear about what she needed, and she was clear about the fact that she could not work for less. She also made it clear that her position was in line with the realities of the marketplace. This is neither aggressiveness nor passivity. It's assertiveness. Sharon did her research, was confident about the facts, and was able to state her position very clearly. If you do this honestly and convincingly, there's a good chance you can prevent a conflict from getting started. If conflict does start, you can keep it from escalating or bring it quickly to an end.

HOW TO CONDUCT YOURSELF WHEN IN CONFLICT

If do you find yourself in conflict, think of how small children behave when they're arguing in the sandbox, and don't act like that! Don't call people names. Don't point fingers. Don't try to paint yourself as completely blameless at the expense of the other party. Those tactics only increase self-justification and defensiveness by the other side. Talk about your own behavior rather than anyone else's. If you're feeling impatient, it's much better to say "I'm going to wait until you're finished talking" than "Why don't you stop talking already?" It's not always easy to show that kind of restraint, but it's much more productive in the long run.

Another key point: Keep the focus on the present or the future. Don't get hung up on the past. Invoking what happened last week or last year is almost always a bad idea in business conflicts, regardless of the point you're trying to make. Often people refer to past successes as a way of getting what they want now: "Look at all I've done for this company in the last year! You can't treat me like this now!" All that may be true, of course, but it's essentially a sentimental argument. As we've said, both the good thing and the bad thing about business relationships is that they're basically unsentimental. Business friendships are mainly significant when everything is going well. When problems arise in the workplace, it's amazing how fast good buddies can become strangers.

Instead of talking about the past, emphasize what you can contribute now and in the future, provided this conflict is brought to a satisfactory end. This is your real bargaining chip. This is how you can show that it's in everyone's best interests if your needs are met. On the other hand, if you can't present yourself as a valuable asset to the future of the organization, your position is greatly weakened. So always be aware of what the company really needs, and why those needs can't possibly be met without your contribution.

Also on the subject of the past, avoid using certain words and phrases that tend to perpetuate ongoing problems and drag them into the present situation. If the discussion gets heated, for example, you might find yourself telling someone, "You always do that" or "You never fail to act that way." These kinds of negative descriptions and generalizations tend to be self-fulfilling. In trying to resolve a conflict, it's much better to be aware of any positive changes, however small, and reinforce them.

One of the most important instances of this principle occurred during the Cuban missile crisis of 1962. As you may know, this was the closest the world has ever come to an atomic war, with the United States and the Soviet Union facing off over the presence of Russian nuclear missiles in Cuba. At one point, the United

States received what seemed to be a positive message from the Russians, suggesting a way that the conflict could be resolved. While President Kennedy and his advisers were studying the message, a second communication arrived, which was much more hard line. At this point, Kennedy made a brilliant move. He decided to respond immediately to the first message and ignore the second one. By reinforcing the positive rather than focusing on the negative, the world was literally saved. So remember this principle. It's assertive, and it's effective.

Finally, and perhaps most importantly, let's look on the bright side. Let's envision a scenario in which you have successfully brought the conflict to a resolution. In fact, let's assume that your needs have been met and that in conventional terms you could be considered the "winner" of the dispute. At this point, it's very important that you resist any temptation to do a dance in the end zone, as it were. If you don't leave the other party an honorable retreat, you can be certain the conflict will reignite at some point. Next time the outcome might not be so favorable, though. As we mentioned, this was something Lincoln understood as the Civil War drew to a close, and there was never again an open conflict between the states. It was something the Allies failed to understand at the end of World War One, and the result was economic catastrophe and the rise of Adolf Hitler.

If you fail to be gracious at the end of a conflict in a business setting, you may not turn the other party into a fascist dictator, but you'll almost certainly come to regret your behavior. After all, the purpose of assertive conflict resolution is not a "win" but an "all-win." When you keep that in mind, you'll take a big step toward mastering people skills, not just mastering people.

NONVERBAL COMMUNICATION

So far in our discussion of conflict resolution, we've focused mostly on what is said. We've emphasized what to say and not to say. But the truth is that 90 percent of a human interaction takes place through nonverbal communication. This includes facial expressions, gestures, and body language in general. It can also include your choice of clothing, what you order for lunch, or whether you're late or early for a meeting.

People tend to react more to what we *think* someone means than what they meant to say or actually say. This is especially true in conflict situations. For this reason, you need to pay just as much attention to your nonverbal signals as you do to your words. Body language is especially important in this respect. In fact, the power of body language is so strong that it can create trust or erode it almost instantly. So make no mistake: Good nonverbal communication is a critical skill for conflict resolution.

On the most obvious level, positive body language means smiling, making eye contact, and standing neither too close nor too far away from another person. But there's more to it than that. When you match or mirror the postures, gestures, and tone of voice of the other party, their brain receives some very reassuring signals. The message that your mirroring language suggests is, "Hey, this person is just like me." Since people trust those who are most like them, you can think of nonverbal communication as a kind of dance. You are the follower, but by following well, you'll actually be able to take the lead. Once again, this is a good way to both prevent conflict and bring it to a positive resolution.

Remember, the key is always to be as subtle and discreet as possible. The purpose of mirroring, for example, is not to mimic precisely what the other person is doing. It's not a matter of scratching your head whenever they do. Rather, it's putting them at ease by trying to capture the meaning of their actions, while keeping your intention outside their conscious awareness.

Let's look at some specific techniques for achieving this result. First, keep yourself in sync by making sure that your body language, your words, and your tone of voice all match. Suppose someone is telling you how sorry he is about a perceived insult.

You might be gratified by what he's saying, but what if his arms are tightly crossed against his chest? What if his eyes are rolling as he speaks? What if his whole nonverbal message is that he still thinks you're an enormous pain in the butt? In that case, the positive meaning of his words is a lot less assertive than the negativity of everything else.

Second, when you're speaking forcefully with another person, maintain eye contact without staring or glaring, and don't forget to blink! To see how important this is, try looking in the mirror while just slightly squinting your eyes or looking off to the side. Even the smallest difference has a huge effect on how you're perceived.

Third, assess the atmosphere and spirit of the interaction, and match the other person's energy. Stand, walk, or sit just as they do. Do they walk fast or slow? Do they lean toward you in their chair or incline away from you? Then gradually adapt your positions so that they match or mirror the other person. As we've said, don't make this too obvious. It's not a game of charades. It's using a basic people skill with subtlety and taste. In addition to matching gestures, match tone of voice as well. Voice tone is comprised of three elements: high or low pitch, fast or slow speed, and loud or soft volume. If the people around you are speaking in quiet tones, or more emphatically, you should do the same.

Fourth, make an effort to sound positive and enthusiastic, even if the discussion gets heated. People are always influenced by positive energy. Difficult though it may be, assertive conflict resolution means smiling and looking confident no matter what. If you start to feel uncontrollably hostile, take a deep breath or ask for a glass of water. Make a focused effort to improve your mood.

Fifth, if you know you're going to have a meeting in which conflict may arise, make sure you're dressed appropriately. Even before you say anything, wearing the wrong clothes can be extremely insulting. On the other hand, you can again use the mirroring principle simply by dressing as the situation requires.

Next, pay special attention to the importance of the handshake. This is a time-honored gesture that has deep resonance in our culture, especially in terms of conflict resolution. After all, the original intention of a handshake was to show that the parties were not hiding knives in their hands! In general, a firm handshake is an especially assertive sign, and it is a significant gesture when sealing deals and resolving conflict.

Finally, after any meeting in which conflict has surfaced, it's a very good idea to write by hand a brief and sincere note to the other party in a positive and conciliatory tone. Do this win, lose, or draw. A note like this is not just a communication. It's actually a gift, and when you give someone a gift, they tend to respond in kind.

Above all, remember that conflict resolution is mostly based on intention. You know in your heart when you're ready to stop fighting. When you feel that impulse, don't let your ego prevent you from responding to it. By the same token, be alert for signs in the other party that they're ready to move in the direction of resolution. Often these signs are very small and subtle, but don't ignore them. Assertive conflict resolution means picking up on any positive sign and making the most of it.

ACTION STEPS

1. The account of how Lincoln humbly apologized to James Shields for the letters that were published in the newspaper is powerful. He clearly took responsibility, and seeing the errors of his ways, humbly apologized. Reflect on your career. Have you been willing to accept full responsibility for any errors that had been made by you or your team? Make a list of those past errors that you hold yourself accountable for. If there is something you need to own up to, it's never too late. After doing so, make the commitment to take full responsibility for your action.

2. When dealing with conflict, there are steps you can take to make the experience as pleasant and productive as possible. The next time you have to work out a conflict, go through the steps below and put an X in the boxes where you need to improve your skills and a check by the areas in which you were effective.

☐   Make an honest assessment of the nuts and bolts of a situation.

☐   Include your needs in the assessment.

☐   Avoid rhetoric that attacks the other. This will only create defensiveness in their response.

☐   Talk about your behavior over someone else's.

☐   Focus only on the present and future. Don't dig up past incidents.

☐   Watch your nonverbal body language. Remain in an open, responsive stance, and avoid folding your arms or leaning away from the interaction. These are signs of defensiveness and closed-mindedness.

☐   No matter what the outcome, end on a gracious and hospitable note.

3. Write a list of internal struggles or conflict that you are currently facing. Then write out the action steps that you need to take to resolve them. When possible, give yourself a deadline. Then take a breath and acknowledge yourself for being so courageous and proactive.

ACTION PLAN NOTES

When we're angry with other people, enemies, we are giving them power over us: power over our sleep, our appetites, our blood pressure, our health, and our happiness. Our enemies would dance with joy if only they knew how they were worrying us, lacerating us, and getting even with us! Our anger hurts them not at all, but it turns our own days and nights into turmoil.

—Dale Carnegie

CHAPTER 16

Assertive Conflict Management and Negotiation

Here in the final chapter of the book we'll conclude our discussion of assertive conflict resolution. We'll see how this really connects with some other topics that are extremely important, not only for your career success but for your life as a whole.

Every day, you're involved in many situations of potential conflict. You constantly find yourself in settings in which your wants and needs are not the same as some other person's. In fact, since no two people are exactly alike, virtually every circumstance of your life falls into this category of experience. In all these situations where your desires differ from someone else's, there are three possible outcomes.

First, you might emerge as the "winner." You might get

everything you want, while the other person gets nothing. However, the reverse might take place as well. You could be the "loser." The other person's objectives are met and yours aren't.

In the real world, a complete win for either party is rare. Usually the result falls somewhere in between. There's give-and-take, and some form of compromise is reached. The situation is resolved, and the means by which this happens is negotiation. In a negotiated situation, there are conflicts of interests. Often what one person wants isn't exactly what the other wants. Usually both sides prefer to search for solutions, rather than giving in, walking away, or simply getting furiously angry at one another.

Negotiation, therefore, is the name we give to conflict resolution by means other than mere interpersonal warfare. Let's look at strategies and tactics of effective negotiation, which is, after all, the medium through which conflict resolution takes place.

MANAGING CONFLICT

Few people actually enjoy being in conflict with other human beings. Conflicts with supervisors, subordinates, or coworkers are not pleasant experiences, especially if the conflict becomes hostile. Negotiating a solution to conflict can be mentally exhausting and emotionally draining. The process can be made easier, however, by keeping your eye on the potential benefits. An effective negotiation can be a highly positive experience both personally and professionally. The key from the outset is to identify the conflict and manage it rather than letting it spin out of control. In that way, the path can be made clear for a negotiated solution. When a conflict of interests exists, don't deny it, but don't escalate it either. Commit to and hold a positive attitude about negotiating it. In itself, your commitment is an assertive people skill, and it should be the strong foundation of your approach to conflict resolution.

If you're like many people, you may seek to avoid conflict when it arises, or deny it. A better alternative is using conflict as a setting for your creative and assertive people skills. The modern corporation is becoming less based on titles and official power. There are fewer clear boundaries of responsibility and authority. As a result, conflict or potential conflict will be an even greater presence in the workplace of the future. Negotiation skills, therefore, can be a huge element in your career success. Moreover, there are some very specific and very powerful techniques that can quickly make you an effective negotiator, starting today.

Skilled negotiators begin with a key concept in mind. They know that it's important to satisfy their own needs, but they also see the value in satisfying the other party. The goal is for you to feel that the conflict has been successfully resolved, and for the other person to feel that way also. In short, you need to aim for an all-win outcome. The magic of a good negotiation is creating a "win-win" situation even if it looks like a "win-lose." The truth is, almost all negotiations have at least some elements of win-win. The trick is to find them.

To help you do that, let's look at three fundamental strategic principles.

First, make a commitment to an all-win approach.

Second, clarify what you want and why you want it.

And finally, have a focused picture of your "Plan B," or walkaway position. That is, the circumstances in which you'll need to end the negotiation without a resolution. Although this may seem like a worst-case scenario, assertive people skills will keep it from being no worse than it has to be.

As a leader, try to refrain from viewing negotiation as a competitive endeavor in which you have to make a killing in order to emerge the "winner." Even a so-called failed negotiation can be a stepping-stone to forming relationships that can have long-term benefits for you and your company. In this sense, negotiation never really ends. One piece of failed negotiation can often be the start of the next phase.

Each of these principles is essential to resolving conflict in a business setting, and now we'll look at them in detail.

Your Mind-set Is Key

As you begin the negotiation process, the mind-set you bring to the experience is critically important. You must begin with the assumption that a win-win solution exists and that your task is to reveal it. Even if you have serious doubts about this deep in your heart, you must convince yourself that it's true. In other words, you must place the responsibility for a positive outcome on your own shoulders, rather than on external circumstances or on the other party. This may seem like a tall order, but seeing yourself as the controlling factor is actually far preferable to putting your fate in someone else's hands. So make your mind-set positive, and make self-determination the basis of that mind-set. You're in control, and you're going to assert that control in a way that will be good for everyone.

You have a much better chance of a win-win if you approach the negotiation with this sense of self-empowerment. From that perspective, it will be much easier to show your interest in the other side's concerns, and your determination to find a win-win resolution. You can do this by trying to create alternatives that have high value to the other person, by phrasing options in ways that align with the other person's interests, or even by allowing your opponent to declare victory.

Generally speaking, there are two personality types among leaders, and their different characteristics determine their negotiating style. Autocratic leaders hold the view that they should get what they want when they interact with team members. Why? Simply because of their title and the hierarchy of the organization. Their routine response might be "Because I'm the boss." They may think they're negotiating, but what they're really interested in doing is giving orders.

In the process of handing out orders, autocratic leaders don't realize the extent to which they may be antagonizing others. Even when the tasks they assign are completed, they may be carried out improperly or inefficiently. This is the phenomenon known as "malicious obedience," in which an order is technically fulfilled but subtly undermined at the same time. For instance, imagine an autocratic leader who sends his assistant out to get him a sandwich for lunch. The assistant comes back with a ham sandwich, and the manager yells: "You call this a lunch? Get me something decent to eat!" So the assistant goes to a five-star restaurant and gets a take-out lunch for five hundred dollars. Technically, he's followed the order, but he's also used his obedience to aggress against the authority. Like "buyer's remorse" in the world of sales, malicious obedience is a frequent occurrence in negotiations with an autocratic personality.

The Accommodating Personality

A second negotiating type is the accommodating personality, which may be either a leader or a subordinate. Regardless of their status in the organization, they're more concerned with what others want than with their own needs. Sometimes in order to avoid conflict, they don't negotiate at all and end up sabotaging their own interests. Since negotiation implies conflict, it's critical for these people to force a certain amount of compromise. This is the only way they can become effective participants in a business enterprise.

ADOPTING THE COLLABORATIVE MIND-SET

Suppose you were going into a negotiation with either of the two personalities we've just described. What mind-set would you want to adopt? Would it be positive or negative? Collaborative or confrontational? If you were dealing with an autocratic individual, would you let her set the stage for malicious obedience on your part? Would your hidden agenda be to win a guerrilla war against the big bully, by letting him at first think he's won? Or, if you were facing an extremely accommodating person, would you want to take advantage of that person's perceived weakness for your own benefit? In the short term, there might be a certain satisfaction in these hostile intentions on your part, but they would not really be assertive in the sense that we've been using the term. You might have asserted yourself against your adversary, but you have not asserted yourself against your own negative impulses. You have not entered the negotiation with a positive mind-set. A positive mind-set means seeing what is positive in the other person and in the situation as a whole, and maximizing that positive element. True, it may not be easy to deal with some of the extreme personalities we've just described. Assertive people skills often aren't easy, at least in the short term. But, in the long run, using them well makes life much easier for everyone.

It is critical to understand that negotiating cannot be learned by following a prepackaged set of behaviors and applying them to all situations. That might work if everyone could be counted on to behave rationally and predictably. But they can't, because people are often emotional and irrational. To negotiate well, you must prepare to use a variety of approaches depending on who's on the other side of the table. The key word here is *prepare*. You need to prepare by knowing what you want and what the other person wants. Prepare for the other person's potentially abrasive or submissive behavior. And prepare to take responsibility for turning those elements into a win-win resolution.

Most important, be clear about your real goals and real issues, and try honestly to identify the other person's real needs. Many negotiations fail because people are primarily worried about being taken advantage of. They lose sight of the authentic issues. They're more concerned about whether the other side won or might have taken even a step in the direction of winning. This is a fundamentally weak approach, although it may try to portray itself as strength.

BE CLEAR ABOUT YOUR WANTS AND NEEDS

This is our second strategic principle. After first committing yourself to a win-win outcome, be clear about what you want and why you want it. And make a distinction between your real wants and needs and those that are just serving some superficial intention. Don't focus on the size or shape of the table, because that's not what the negotiation is really about.

Third, be clear about the circumstances in which you would have to walk away from the negotiation. Or, to put it another way, are there any situations in which you would walk away?

If there aren't, there should be, because in any serious negotiation you must be prepared to break off if you see that your real needs can't be met. If you have $200,000 with which to buy a house, and the seller wants $400,000, you can certainly begin an assertive negotiation. You can find many side issues to discuss and perhaps concessions will be made on either side. If the seller continues to demand twice as much money as you've got, however, you must be prepared to walk away.

On the other hand, if you really and truly don't have a walk-away situation, and the other party is a determined negotiator, you can save everyone time by simply giving in at the outset.

Let's return to the example of the house. Suppose you walk away from the seller who wanted $400,000, and you find a seller who wants $200,000 (exactly the amount of money you have). But now a new thought strikes you. Maybe you should buy a house for $100,000 instead of spending every penny you have.

Your conversation with the seller might go something like this: "I like the house you're offering for two hundred thousand dollars, but I'm wondering if I can get just as good a house for one hundred thousand dollars. So I think I'll look around for a while."

"Well," says the seller, "you can look around all you want, but I can assure you there are no houses like this for one hundred thousand dollars."

Despite this, you decide to explore the market. You want a three-bedroom house with a two-car garage and a swimming pool. Those are your real needs in the situation, but as you look around, it begins to appear that the seller was right. There don't seem to be any houses like that for $100,000. If you want to be stubborn about it, you can keep looking in a wider and wider area. You can wait and see what other houses come on the market. Maybe you could even wait for years. The truth is, if you really and truly need that three-bedroom house and there are no others available, you actually have no walkaway position and you will have to meet the seller's price. If that's the case, you might as well do it sooner rather than later. If you don't, you're not being tough. You're just being stubborn.

BE CLEAR ABOUT YOUR PLAN B

A useful concept here is always having a Plan B when you go into a negotiation—that is, the course you will take if you absolutely cannot reach an agreement. If you're negotiating over salary, for example, your alternatives might include a specific job elsewhere, a longer job search, or remaining at your current job. This is a crucial reference point because your walkaway, or Plan B, establishes a threshold for the settlement. The outcome of the negotiation needs to match or do better than your Plan B.

Determining your Plan B, or walkaway position, is not always easy. You have to establish a concrete value for various alternatives. For instance, you know the value of your current job, but would it be worthwhile to take a $5,000 salary hike that involves moving to a new city? In simple negotiations, there may be just one issue like this. Often, though, there are many variables that can make your walkaway point very elusive. What's more, it's almost equally important to determine the other party's walkaway or Plan B. In fact, one goal of assertive negotiation could be to come as close to the other person's walkaway as you can.

If and when you truly do arrive at your Plan B, here are some things you'll need to keep in mind. In most conflict situations in a corporate setting, you'll have a continuing relationship with the other person, so don't leave the bargaining table with a gloomy attitude, and don't let the other party do that either. Again, it's not easy, but look at this as a test of your assertiveness and your people skills. By doing so, you'll open up the possibility for a better outcome at a later date.

Here's an example of how this can work. Kim and Gretchen are both freelance graphic designers. A small publishing company had decided to bring out a new line of cookbooks, which would be very design intensive. Kim and Gretchen were both hired to work on the new line. Although they don't know each other, they negotiated deals for themselves that came out to just about the same amount of money. Both of them were really excited about the new project. They were also gratified to get personal calls from Paul, the editorial director of the publishing company, who told them how great it made him feel to give them this break.

That was on a Friday. On the following Monday, the phone rang again in Kim's studio, and in Gretchen's also. This time it wasn't Paul. It was his assistant, who told the two designers that over the weekend Paul had thought about the new project and had decided to cancel it. He was sorry, but that was his decision, and thanks for your time.

Kim was instantly furious. First she gave Paul's assistant an earful, and then she quickly wrote an email to Paul himself. She told him that it had been extremely unprofessional to commit to something and then to suddenly back out of it. She mentioned that she had put other work on hold in order to keep herself available for this project, and now she had probably lost that business as well. Finally, she pointed out how gutless it was of Paul to make his assistant deliver the bad news. From a purely factual point of view, Kim was correct in just about everything she said.

Gretchen was also angry when she got the call from Paul's assistant, but she knew that moments like this are the test of a professional's people skills. She spoke briefly but politely with the assistant, and then, like Kim, she wrote an email to Paul. She disciplined herself to express her appreciation for the opportunity, as well as her disappointment that it was not going to take place. And she closed with the hope that even though this didn't come through, perhaps there would be another project down the road.

What was the outcome of this episode? First, within a year Paul was gone from the publishing company. His former assistant took over his job, and one of his first acts was to sign Gretchen on for some major new work. He thought of calling Kim as well, but she had seemed so angry that he was sure she wouldn't want to work with him.

In a walkaway situation, it is critical to address future possibilities, not current problems, and definitely not personalities. Resist the temptation to attack anyone personally. If the dialogue starts taking place on that level, people will just defend their self-esteem. Try to maintain a rational frame of mind oriented toward your long-term goals. If necessary, let the other blow off steam without your taking it personally. Make it clear that you know the conflict is about the issues, and it's not personal. This will help to prevent the other side from feeling angry and defensive both now and when future opportunities come up.

CULTIVATING SOME OF THE INTANGIBLES IN NEGOTIATION

Beside the explicit strategies we've discussed, there are many intangibles that can influence the negotiation of a conflict. Subtle verbal and body language can make a difference in how the resolution progresses. Spend more time listening than talking and make direct eye contact. Use the word *and* instead of *but*. Using *but* discounts everything that was said previously, whereas using *and* sends the message that you're interested in the other party and are seeking common ground.

More specifically, be very careful about using the phone, email, and other nonvisual communication vehicles. A lack of facial expressions, vocal intonation, and other face-to-face cues can result in huge misunderstandings. Again and again, reiterate your interest in the other side's concerns and your determination to find a mutually satisfactory resolution.

Sometimes the location where the negotiation takes place can be important. Is it happening in a space where you or the other party is uncomfortable? Are you in a location that is perhaps too comfortable? In an office environment, there's always the sense that things have to go through official channels, and people have to live up to their reputations. If possible, go outside for a coffee or even just a walk around the block. As a general rule, anything is better than meeting in someone's carefully constructed personal fortress.

If you have had previous experience in conflict resolution with this person, be aware of how this history might affect the present situation. If it was a positive experience, frame the new interaction in that context. If it was negative, find a way of starting fresh if that's possible. Otherwise consider asking someone else to handle the negotiation on your behalf. Be aware that people place very different importance on elements of a conflict. For example, in negotiating for a job, you may place a high value on location and less on salary, or vice versa. Be mindful of your subjective viewpoints, and try to ascertain the other party's also. Knowing what is really "valued" (not just quantified) is a big part of assertive conflict resolution.

Always be aware of time pressure as well. If there isn't any, create some. In a business or corporate negotiation, every step in conflict resolution should have a "what by when" time frame attached to it. Otherwise, the principle of work expanding to fill the time available will take hold. Even if it takes forever!

Finally, here's a thought that applies not only to conflict resolution but to all the people skills we've discussed in these chapters. It comes from Roger Fisher, a former professor at Harvard, and the coauthor of *Getting to Yes*, one of the best-selling negotiation books of all time. Roger Fisher said, "Be unconditionally constructive. Approach a conflict with this attitude: 'I accept you as an equal negotiating partner; I respect your right to differ; I will be receptive.' Some criticize my approach as being too soft. But negotiating by these principles are a sign of strength."

Each day and each week, all of us engage in many interactions, but that does not mean we become better at it. To become better we need awareness of the structure and dynamics of people skills. We need to think clearly, objectively, and critically. Above all, we need to act assertively.

There is no one "best" style of assertive people skills. You'll need to find the tools and techniques that are most effective for you. Try out the ideas we've explored in these chapters, and see what works best. A few ideas quoted by Dale Carnegie come as close as possible to being universal principles. Here they are.

Have unlimited patience. Never corner other people, and always assist them in saving face. In order to see through other people's eyes, put yourself in their shoes. Avoid self-righteousness like the devil. And above all, take action. Inaction breeds doubt and fear. Action breeds confidence and courage. If you want to conquer the negative elements in your life, don't sit at home and think about it. Go out and get busy!

ACTION STEPS

1. Having keen negotiating skills can advance you in your career. First, based on the information given, make a list

of all the traits that a good negotiator would have. Then make note of all of the listed traits that you possess. Make a concerted effort to develop and practice those traits that you do not possess. Then keep a journal of the changes and results that you note in response to enhancing your skill set.

2. The three fundamental strategic principles to power negotiating are

    1. Commitment to an all-win approach.

    2. Clarifying what you want and why you want it.

    3. Be ready with a focused picture of your Plan B, or walkaway position. Find a friend or coworker with whom you can practice these strategies. Do some mock negotiating with your partner, each taking honest notes, of the other's strengths and opportunities for improvement. Enjoy this exercise and take note of the positive shifts that you make as you practice these techniques.

3. During a conflict, focusing your attention on finding a way to satisfy the other while still taking care of your needs puts you in a very powerful position. Getting out of the way, however, takes a great deal of discipline, consciousness, and practice. The next time you enter into a negotiation or conflict situation, consciously choose to focus on the needs of the other before engaging. Once it is resolved, be sure to write about any insights that you have gained by shifting your position from yourself to the service of someone else. Most often the results are quite extraordinary!

ACTION PLAN NOTES

About the Author

Dale Carnegie was born in 1888 in Missouri. He wrote his now-renowned book *How to Win Friends and Influence People* in 1936—a milestone that cemented the rapid spread of his core values across the United States. During the 1950s, the foundations of Dale Carnegie Training® as it exists today began to take form. Dale Carnegie himself passed away soon after in 1955, leaving his legacy and set of core principles to be disseminated for decades to come.

Today, Dale Carnegie Training includes as its clients four hundred of the Fortune 500 companies. With a roster of more than seven million graduates, Dale Carnegie Training is dedicated to serving the business community worldwide.

For more information, please visit www.dalecarnegie.com.

DALE CARNEGIE®
TRAINING

ABOUT DALE CARNEGIE TRAINING®

Dale Carnegie partners with middle market and large corporations, as well as organizations, to produce measurable business results by improving the performance of employees with emphasis on:

- leadership
- sales
- customer service
- presentations
- team member engagement
- process improvement

Recently identified by *The Wall Street Journal* as one of the top 25 high-performing franchises, Dale Carnegie Training programs are available in more than 25 languages throughout the entire United States and in more than 80 countries.

Dale Carnegie's corporate specialists work with individuals, groups and organizations to design solutions that unleash your employees' potential, enabling your organization to reach the next level of performance. Dale Carnegie Training offers public courses, seminars and workshops, as well as in-house customized training, corporate assessments, online reinforcement and one-on-one coaching.

For more information, please visit www.dalecarnegie.com.